EVERYDAY PRESENCE

– a personal description –

Coverdesign and Illustrations by Emma Ekstam http://emmaekstam.com/

Covertypeface: *Brioche* by Jessica Hische

Inlay: Aninia Schwanhäußer

Forlag: Books on Demand GmbH, København, Danmark

Tryk: Books on Demand GmbH, Norderstedt, Tyskland

ISBN 978-8-7718-8276-6

„People need time to deal with the now before it runs away and becomes the then."

Terry Pratchett

Aninia Schwanhäußer

EVERYDAY PRESENCE

– a personal description –

Books on Demand

INTRODUCTION

When I started writing this book, I was missing a description of body awareness that is both related to everyday life and based on a *real* person's experience. I was missing an example of how someone who is practicing body attention, actually integrates this into their *everyday life*, and what it means for them to be present or aware. I was looking for an opportunity to follow someone's thinking, without being told what this is supposed to mean for my own life.

If you're reading this book, I assume that you are in one way or another interested in the subject of self-development, presence, the body and attention. You might be a student or a practitioner, a person looking for a personal practice for presence or even a critic of self-development. Maybe you're developing your own movement practice of sorts. Or you're generally interested in people, and with a kind of anthropological mindset you observe how people around you conceptualize their lives. Either way, I assume that you're not looking for a solution or a quick fix for your life by reading this book, but that you're interested in following another person's thinking process.

As I didn't find anything like this in my own search for a down to earth approach where I don't have to buy into a spiritual belief-system first – I decided to take a shot at it myself and share an example. This is a very personal description of how I conceptualize my practice of paying attention to the body. How I practice being present in everyday life.

You will find personal definitions of terms that are sometimes used in everyday life and sometimes connected to a specific field. What I'm trying is to share with you is **my definition**, how I apply and integrate those terms or concepts in my thinking process and life. And this is what they are meant to be. Personal definitions in a process. So this is not a book of exercises, but an attempt to describe my philosophy of life – share with you *my* current belief system for reality, if you so will.

Some background on why I am interested in the subject of presence and practicing attention to the body in the first place:

Coming from both theater and a so-called alternative background (with an awareness for feelings, a psychosomatic nature of things, importance of arts and relationships etc.), I still ended up burned out when I was only 25 years old. In addition with an already previously experienced discomfort with a dissonance between concepts of presence on stage or in my training room and just everyday life, this created a strong motivation to invest in learning something new...

Since then, I have been looking for ways to train presence and integration of the body in everyday life as well as in extraordinary situations. I've been looking for and experimenting with ways to integrate the energy and attention of excitement, fear or uncertainty, and to deal with pain or unexpected circumstances more sustainably – in everyday life. A question I had and continuously carry with me, is how to live intensely (connecting to people on a personal level, daring new things, confronting things I disagree with, being vulnerable with others) without burning out myself or others. Thus, how can I stay present in everyday life?

I'm the Expert... on *my* experience

There are so many methods in the world, so many people who have found the way or express some kind of certainty. I have met many charismatic, knowledgeable people. Many opinions, approaches or methods to achieve one thing: living well and enjoying it. **Being authentic**. Many of them gave me the impression that their way of living well and enjoying it, is the best way. Or the most knowledgeable way. Or the most logical way. Or the right way. Or the most valuable way of them all – whatever that's supposed to mean.

Something in this has been annoying me. I get angry when someone claims a general truth. Not just one way of describing things, but this is how it is for **people**. I guess this is true not only for finding ways of living well but in general – when someone talks with certainty about how the world works.

> *This is what you need to do to live well.*

> *This is how you stop smoking and how you heal your belly.*

> *You should follow your passion.*

> *You should do what you love.*

> *The five steps to becoming an empathic leader.*

> *When the stars are positioned like this – this very specific energy will influence your work-life.*

> *Our brains aren't adapted to today's level of stress but kind of stuck in some pre-industrial time.*

> *The best thing in the world is to dance Salsa. No Ballet. No Lindy Hop.*

> *No, dance freely, just follow your heart.*

Somehow, they're all saying you have to find your own way. And at the same time, that their way is the best...

I believe that most people are basically looking for a way of living well. For navigating smoothly in the inevitable paradoxes we encounter. Some way of enjoying life – whether that is around pleasure or fulfilling a duty or something totally different.

I also know the experience of relief when something is described simply and with clarity. This kind of relief might be what makes it so tempting to describe cause-and-effect-equations that provide a kind of recipe to making life simpler.

I believe each living being has their own life with their own challenges and solutions.

I believe living is complex – way too complex to fit into simple solutions. Many – sometimes paradoxical, – things happen simultaneously, and I won't ever be able to consciously notice or acknowledge all of them at once.

And here I come now and say I have found ways to still be present and navigate in this complex reality – ways that I'm excited and happy about. Writing this down, and finding my own words for it, I also notice how tempting it is to talk about the truth. How tempting to say something like „Everyday Presence is the way to live an interesting and easy life – even in intensity".

But I actually don't think it is.

Discovering the concepts and practices that I share here, happened through my own experiences. Some of these experiences took place in structured learning environments like my professional training as a practitioner of a body based training of attention and somatic bodywork, my dance classes or other workshops. And many of them in the adaptation outside of school – rock climbing, dealing with relationships and friends, building my own stable foundation in a new country. This experiential way has been the most fun and effective form of learning for me. Sometimes, of course, it is frustrating - but which learning process isn't, at one point or another?

When I participate in such experiential learning environments, I experience learning as strongly connected to my body's way of interacting with the world. In combination with my thinking about those experiences (both in preparation as well as reflection), my physical experience is my strongest learning tool.

It might seem ironic to then write a book and create something less experiential. However, writing has been a way of clarifying for myself how I conceptualize my body, mind, and life in a way that comes from experience instead of coming from theory and mere intellectual understanding. For me, coming from experience means that some things don't need to be logical or can even be paradoxical when I think about them. But having this element of ambivalence as part of my description gives me more peace of mind than trying to create a logical A always leads to B leads to C-explanation of how things work.

I don't believe there is a version of life that we can just copy from someone else, and then we'll be well. Neither is there one process, or concept, that will fit exactly to another person's life. Or one way of training or experiencing presence. How should I know the way? I hardly know what I'm doing right now. Sometimes I can just describe what I perceive...

I have found ways and tools to be more present in everyday life that I enjoy and practice in my current circumstances. I especially enjoy that it feels like I'm really finding my own solutions – sometimes by agreeing to follow what everyone does, sometimes by creating something totally different, sometimes just something slightly weird.

About the structure of this book

In a book, things have to have an order. Something must come first, then comes the next, and the next etc. I see these thoughts like a body: Even if I describe one arm first, and then move towards other areas of the same body, the first arm isn't the prerequisite for the rest of the body. The rest of the body is there at the same time, and I focus on one specific area to be able to communicate and learn about it. In the same way, all chapters are present in me simultaneously, and I experience them as growing at the same time. Not in a harmonic or synchronized fashion, but rather quite randomly and in an uncertain way. Some things are abstract, others I experience as closely connected to a specific story in my life.

I invite you to approach the book in this same way: Read according to your current interests. It might be that you want to read it from page 1 to X, or that you're more curious about one chapter in particular right now. Follow your curiosity.

With **Basic Concepts** I describe the widest frames for me. I realized that they form a base for my thinking and that I apply them in some way to anything I think or talk about.

Basic Practices are more concrete actions and intentions, and I aim to describe and distinguish basic steps that I train in order to gain or ease presence. They are concrete in the way that they for me are practical and applicable to the body on a very physical level. At the same time, they are practices of attitude and focus that hold an intention, which can be applied to many different concrete activities.

Basic Qualities are again more abstract and combine physical experiences with feelings and attitudes. They are qualities that I associate with Everyday Presence, and the stronger I experience them, the more present and stronger I feel as a whole.

Basic because even as I write this down, I know there are more details and complexity and this is a beginning. And because in moments when I wish to refocus, I can always return to these basics.

I enter this project with an intention to inspire, and simultaneously with the uncertainty whether it will touch anyone at all. An exciting combination.

As a child or teenager, the fear of using the wrong words or saying something at the wrong moment sometimes scared me so much that I didn't say things at all. I tried to think about something until I was sure that I had the perfect words – which could take a long time. The thing was, that when I held back those imperfect expressions, they were still there in the back of my head creating *noise*. Making me slow in my actions or just creating an atmosphere around me. When I was angry and didn't know how to put it into words, I would sometimes walk around with what my mom called the aura of a bomb, creating a distance to those next to me. This holding back of what I needed to say would go on until I had a headache that made me cry. Only when the pain was that strong was I able to express my anger in words, and it felt like all the built up words were spilling out. This was always a great relief, but also quite an effort to go through. And of course, no guarantee for finding the perfect words after all...

I love how today, words allow me to create clarity or describe the ambiguity I experience, and I continue looking for ways of becoming more and more free in my expression. I use words more playfully and with more pleasure, as they are each just the next move in a flow of interaction with the world. And like in any other form of movement, each single move can make the difference, so it is relevant and interesting to pay attention to their effect on me and my surroundings.

I'm quite aware that what I'm writing about is just my way of making sense of my life. And I don't even know if the things I do intentionally are the actual reasons for my life going the way it does. But I enjoy the writing and in the process of creating structure and clarity developing some sort of inner logic. A year from now, I may have learned something new and may describe things in a different way.

Let's see where all of this will go in the end.

This is my way today – use what inspires you, change what needs change and leave out anything that is bullshit.

Aninia

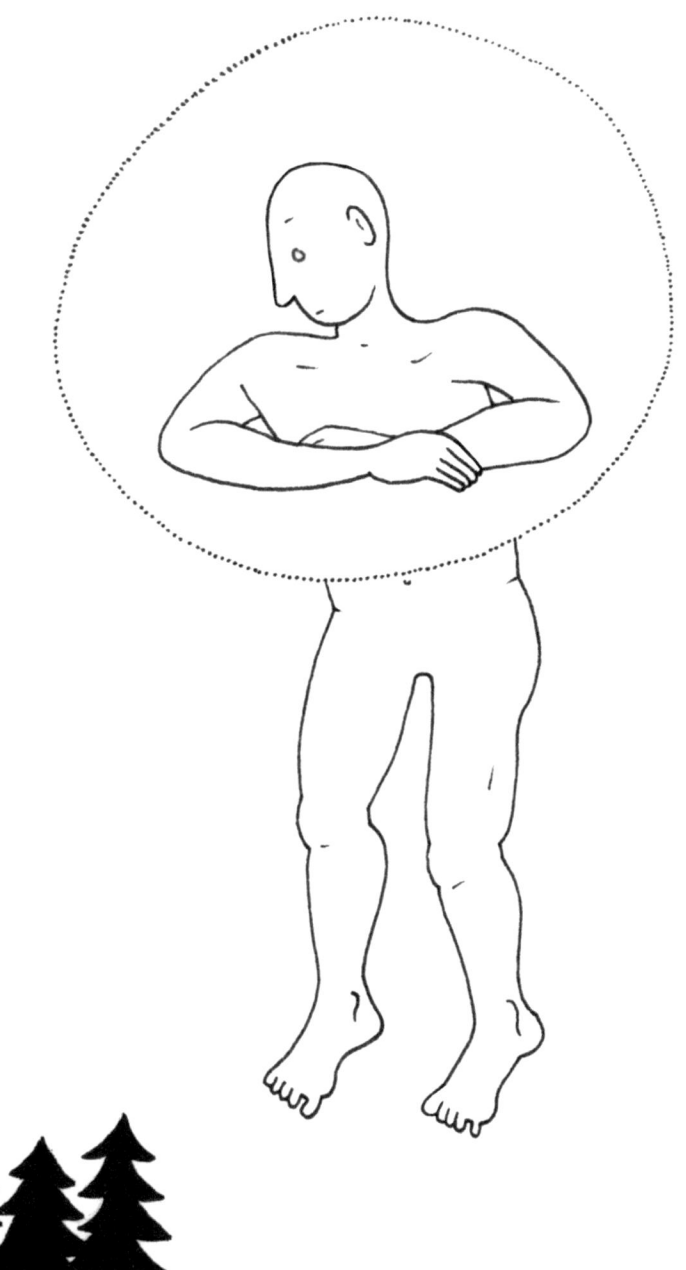

Overview

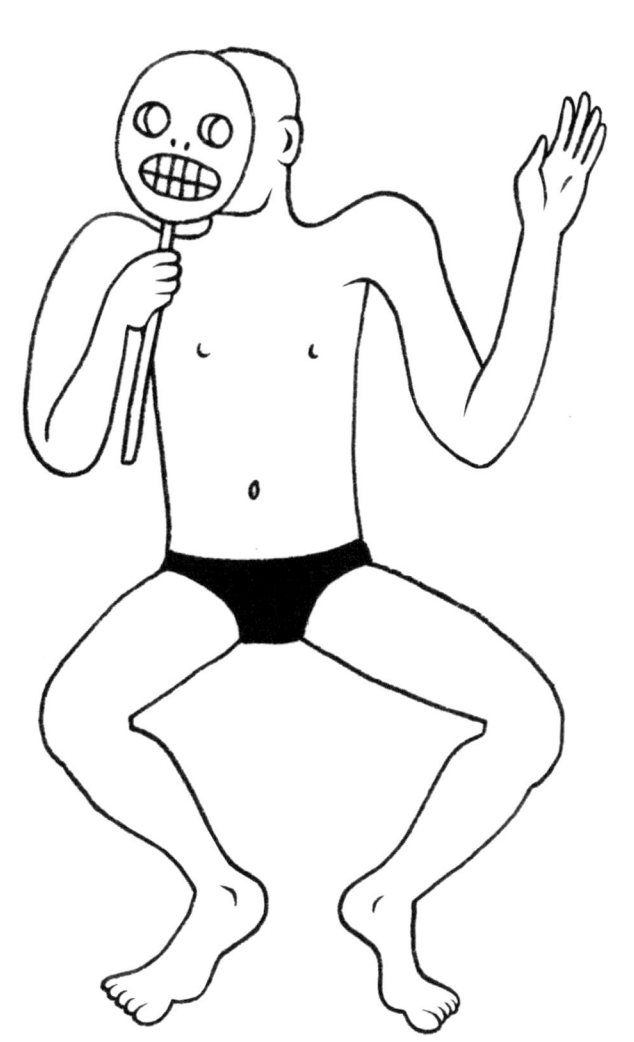

ON PRESENCE

To me, **presence** can be the perfect word to describe the experience of now.

Presence is something that I first learnt about in theater. There, you are required to find a way to be strong and authentic on stage. When you achieve or experience this, usually the audience is touched, the room is transformed. Instead of an actor just narrating what is happening and obviously acting, the character becomes alive and the moment is. In my experience, presence enables an interaction between the story and the listener, the actor and the audience, the individual and the environment. I have experienced this myself, playing or watching. It is an amazing experience to be present.

It was clear to all my colleagues in the drama school and any actor I know, that this is something to train. That it doesn't always happen. That it needs practice and it is appreciated as a sensation of incredible energy and creativity, that allows an experience of ease.

I've also met this term in the community of spiritual or mindful people, as well as self-help gurus who promote **being in the moment**. In these contexts, presence often appeared to me as being related to silence. To being still or calm. To taking time away from everything that is noisy in order to create this silence. In *this* context it is also connected to a kind of practice. It seems understood that it requires dedication and training and isn't just happening all the time. But with the same proposed outcome: When you are present, everything is easy.

With this practice of silence as well as with the training for presence on stage, I have observed a dissonance between the experience of presence on stage and the off-stage lives. When presence happens, it is amazing and exhilarating. But in between, there is everyday life, which is... well... everyday life. Including boring, stressful, nice or painful. Everyday life where I easily get distracted or can't see all the options.

It is in the in-between, when I am neither fully present on a stage nor in silent awareness, that most accidents happen – whether they are physical accidents that lead to injuries, or accidentally hurting myself or others through neglect or inattentiveness when I'm talking to them. It is in those moments, after the big moment on stage or my presentation, that I suddenly trip, slide in the curve with my bike or a sentence just slips out, without attention.

This lack of **a concept of presence in living** and everyday life has been disturbing me. The sensation that the experience of everything being easy would be connected only to the special times, the being on stage (in front of everyone) or being in silence (alone). And that growing old inevitably means becoming set in my ways and inflexible, i.e. unable to adapt to each new situation or movement I meet.

So I wanted to explore and challenge this.

Presence.

Powerful, exciting, scary.

This sensation of just being and exploring what will happen next.

Presence as a state of being in which I can be very awake and calm at the same time, notice options around me without an immediate need to act or choose, but just taking the situation in. Where I have the option to follow one of the impulses I perceive, or to refrain from doing so. I can be aware of both myself and others around me.

So, how to be present in situations that are as common as going to the supermarket, having the slightly uncomfortable conversation with a tax officer or participating in a meeting with full attention? How to keep the wonder about what will happen next while exploring this moment, in daily interactions? I ask(ed) myself these kinds of questions a lot, and trying to grasp and describe some of the concepts and practices I live with today led me to writing this book and to its title Everyday Presence.

Does presence make life easy?

I have been asked, how I make life appear so easy. But I wouldn't say that it is – so easy. My interpretation of this question is „how I enjoy and continue, manage to connect with others even if things become challenging at times". How I go on dancing when things don't turn out as I intended, and how I adapt to the new reality without feeling defeated.

To be honest, I do not know.

What I know is that I'm looking for this experience of being present and alive, and follow what I perceive will lead me to keep that alive. Even when I'm watching a TV-series with a friend.

Obviously, I am not constantly present. And while throughout the past 8 years there were moments when I thought I will eventually arrive at a state of constant presence, I am no longer aiming for that. It is a real pleasure sometimes, to just drift off and be without the imperative of being aware. Not to have to connect with everyone and every possibility in the room.

But it is an easier conscious choice for me today, to change my state of being if there is something that I want to be present for. When I notice that I have been unpresent and regret that – for example, in conversation with a friend, I suddenly realize that I don't know what she has been talking about for the last five minutes – I have tools to bring myself back, either for the next conversation or even in this one. What has also made a difference for me was not beating myself up afterwards – or in advance – for not being present, and being honest about it instead.

Instead of wasting time and energy on judgment and self-punishment, I take chances – with everything I do – that I might make a mistake and need to adjust.

Part of being present in everyday life is this: When I am ready to perceive a situation **as it is** instead of trying to pretend (or tell myself) it is as I hope it to be, then I am also ready to deal with the realization that I don't know what will come out of that situation.

As an example: If I want to be friends with someone and tell myself that we are, I might interpret any of their actions in favor of this reality to be true – we're friends. But maybe if I'm honest, we might actually just be in contact with each other, and not in a way that is a friendship for me. Paying attention to these subtle differences and possibilities for failure, mistakes but also surprises and unexpected pleasure, strengthens the sensation of presence.

I don't know yet what I am actually doing, and very often I cannot explain why I do what I do, but I focus on perceiving it as it is instead of being split between how I hope it will be, how I fear it will be, and how it actually is.

This can sometimes be painful or terrifying.

And often just incredibly liberating.

BASIC CONCEPTS

Everyone I know has a body, everybody moves and interacts with the world around them in one way or another. And I assume everyone has some (more or less conscious) concept of what this actually means and what the interactions are comprised of.

Since I am working with terms that are both used in very specific contexts as well as being essential to everyday language, I see a need to define some of the concepts that I currently take for granted. I want to distinguish what I mean and avoid a situation where two people assume they're talking about the same thing when they say body, but actually mean different things.

The urge to define my basic concepts comes from this need for clarity as well as a need to differentiate my approach from a new age, spiritual, *we all know what we're talking about and agree-atmosphere* that I have experienced when I mention attention to the body and presence.

By clarifying my basic concepts, I also hope to offer transparency and to find a way of talking about the body and presence that is practical for everyday life.

Here are my thoughts...

My Body in Contact with the World

The most basic and profound element of human life according to how I approach and experience it, is the body.

As we are so many people with vastly diverse backgrounds and reasons to talk about the body, there are also many different concepts of what it actually is and how it relates to our human experience of life.

I will share a few more general thoughts and then dive into some subchapters. They sometimes appear as separate topics, like the mind, pain, attention etc., but I see them as integral parts of the body.

So, what do I mean, when I talk about my body? And especially, how is the experience of my body related to the world around me?

I approach my body from the inside – how I experience it – in combination with what I know about it theoretically.

My body is my home.

My body is my tool for interacting with the world and expressing thoughts, needs, wishes, feelings, joy, confusion…

My body is my connection to reality. To others, to nature, to time… All of those, I experience in my body. With my body.

Anything that I am, I express with my body. In my body. Through my body.

My body is at the same time a giant, complex receptor for the impulses of the world and the container of my experiences and memories. I perceive the world through my body; my experiences influence and shape my body, while my shape, flexibility etc. influence my perception of the world.

The more precisely I connect my awareness to the experience of my whole body, the more precisely my device for perception can work. The more present I become in my experience, the better I will know how to react to input from the world in a way that benefits my survival and allows me to create and interact with integrity, based on my ideas and needs. For this to fully function and for me to move smoothly through life, I need to both take care of the material that I am as well as of the processes that I contain.

To clarify: I experience my body as having a material component and a process component. The material – flesh, tissue, fluids, bones – has basic needs to survive: Needs of energy, of movement, of rest, of stimulation, of touch. Needs of safety and rhythm as well as disposal and renewal. These needs are provided for through the process component of my body – my ability to digest, to transform energy, to move, to select what to take in and reject, to think, choose and connect to others around me.

MIND

In my experience, the mind is part of the process component of the body. To describe and structure my experience, I engage my mind. I define it as the process of making sense of anything I experience. And that means mostly internally, for myself. Most of the time, it doesn't have to be logical for anyone else.

I have been stumbling over the term mind and especially categorizations or assessments that value the mind as the best or worst thing. **Mind over body** is one direction, **out of the mind into the body** the other. Both make me wonder, because I so strongly experience my mind as part of my body. To say that my mind wins over my body sounds to me like the mind is something external.

Then I wonder what that would be? I don't understand why we need to separate those two as if being opposites or separate, or in which way that would make it easier to cope in life.

To me, it is obvious that we have the ability to intentionally influence our mind. To do so, we do need a body, though. Even if it is to show that I can overcome pain out of choice, I need the body in the first place, to experience the pain. If I will myself into not feeling the pain, I may make one strong statement, but I won't be able to do much else, as all of me is invested in dealing with this pain. Eventually, I may be stiffening the area that was in pain or stop all flow in that direction, and my ability to react presently to the moment decreases. So, I would use my mind to ignore pain – but in doing so, I would also have to do very physical acts that eventually influence more than just the original pain.

On the other hand, to get out of my mind and into my body... I don't want that either. The more I learn to notice what is happening in bodies (both my own and by paying attention to people around me and clients I work with), the clearer my impression of the mind is of being a very essential, physical process, like digestion. While the digestion process is transforming apples, bread, and coffee into nutrition we can ingest, thus into energy that helps me keep running and be well throughout the day, the process of the mind seems to transform feelings, sensations, and other impressions into ideas and models that help me structure my world and move in it.

To clarify the analogy of those two processes: The digestion process involves many areas of the body. Depending on my intake, I need to invest different amounts of time in order to be satiated and satisfied. Also, depending on what I do during the day, I'll need different amounts of food and I am able to digest some things easier than others. But if the digestion doesn't work and becomes painful, few people would tell me that digestion is harmful and that I should **get out of it**. Rather than intentionally trying to stop it because it hurts, we consider that it might need some attention. We suggest finding out how it can work more smoothly and support our well-being instead of being a hassle. Example: When I eat dairy products, which I cannot digest very easily, my body needs more time and struggles to digest, leading to pain and discomfort. Before I knew that it was the milk I couldn't digest, the symptoms and trying many different things to deal took up a lot of my attention; part of me was constantly busy with my digestion.

When I realized the discomfort comes from milk, I could focus on creating the best conditions for my belly to deal with this. I could stop eating milk products. I could focus on relaxing my belly, on breathing more relaxed, and on just feeling the pain, instead of adding extra tension that would increase the discomfort. Eventually digestion would happen. I sometimes eat milk products despite the pain and the possible sensation afterward that they stays inside me for longer than necessary. I know that I'll need some extra time and attention to deal with it at a later point. But sometimes cake with custard is really worth it.

Sometimes my digestion is weird even though I haven't eaten dairy products. Paying attention to what I do in my belly and back, and learning to relax the habitual tension that I can hold there, allows me to distinguish: Did I eat something (pain remains despite relaxation) or did I actually just need to relax?

Now, the equivalent process of the mind: Like it is difficult for me to digest dairy products, I experience difficulties transforming contradicting or indirect communication into something useful. A very basic example of this is someone telling me that my opinion and feedback is important to them and they would like to use it to learn and develop. If at the same time, they refuse to listen to me, or plainly reject it when I voice any sort of criticism it becomes challenging.

In this situation, a lot of my attention and energy is needed for figuring out which of the two messages to follow. I feel slowed down while trying to interpret both what has been said as well as the reality of the reactions. Like with the digestion of milk, it is even harder to develop a model or structure that I can transform into energy or even enjoy and that allows me to act freely when, simultaneously, I contract my lower belly and shoulders. On the other hand, when I relax my low belly, the area around my eyes and my shoulders, my mind becomes much clearer and calmer. When I also have a soft neck, it is much easier to distinguish if there is something I need to act on regarding this communication, or if it is something that I just need to relax with, let pass and breathe through, in order to move and be in life freely. Maybe I need to wait until the other person has figured out what they actually want. Sometimes people might not want to be direct with me, and sometimes I might misunderstand and things clarify over time.

Today, when my mind is not calm, but racing with thoughts or confusing feelings, not able to grasp which structure or sense to focus on, I use the opportunity to pay attention – is there any part of my body that I can relax? Do I need more energy? When I am relaxed physically – have I heard or thought about something, or have I felt something, that I need to take into account and give more time and attention to?

Sometimes learning to understand another person's communication just needs a moment longer. And sometimes taking this extra moment to notice the physical experience allows me to uncover an unclarity that needs to be taken care of in our communication to support the relationship.

So, for me the mind isn't something to get out of. Just as I don't get out of my digestion. Both of them are essential processes for my well-being, my survival and my interaction with my environment.

But **I want to pay attention to my body** and where I create unnecessary tension for the task at hand. I can learn to relax or bring attention to an area. And then I can be less busy with my mind or my digestion and instead integrate them into the experience of being present in what I want to be doing – be that having an intimate conversation with a friend, enjoying an interesting documentary or fully enjoying the dance, the music and the partner in front of me. I need the functions of the mind as well as my digestion to be able to interact in reality, to be able to notice what is going on around me and make sense of it. I need them to have the energy to create plans, strategies, and actions for change, and also to experience the pleasure of just being in situations that I enjoy.

PAIN and FEAR

I consider both pain and fear to be aspects of the human animal body that have a function for our survival. I think the individual experience and reactions to them, especially when pain and fear have become chronic or feel stuck, appear to sometimes offer the opposite sensation, that they're actually a threat to survival. However, if I look at fear as an impulse that tells me to pay attention, for something that is dangerous, it becomes, similarly to the warning function of pain, a force supporting my survival.

While I experience pain to be collecting attention in a specific physical area, fear **diffuses attention** and kind of makes me try to feel and hear everything at once in order to be safe.

When I can relax with the fact that I feel pain, I can pay attention to what is actually needed in order for me to heal or recover.

Physical sensations like pain or numbness (or lack of sensation) are important aspects for taking care of and maintaining myself. Both pain and numbness in any area of my body interrupt the regular flow of information from the outside in and vice versa, limiting my ability to be present and in connection, and thus constituting a first priority of fixing that condition – which can be a material- as well as a process-disturbance. These disturbances may occur due to physical damage from overuse, accidents, illness or shock – there is a need for the injured area to recover, to heal and grow. Pain shows me very clearly where to focus right now and which issue needs solving, in order for other things to feel enjoyable or relevant again.

Sometimes I can hurt from a different pain – like the loss of a person, neglect or another strong emotions. Then the need for recovery of physical tissue might be less prevalent. However, if I listen to it, the pain can still give me a sensation for what is important and help me set priorities. It can make me slower for example; make me take some time to just rest, without having a specific physical area to take care of, but just noticing that I need to rest. As a whole being.

I can leverage pain as a signal, as an entrance to physical attention. Pain or other discomfort may reveal an area to me where I just need **more energy**, or where I encounter reality around me if, for some reason, I was unaware of it earlier.

Pain can also show me something about the boundaries between myself and the space around me. It might simply make me aware of a border or an obstacle. For example, if I hit myself on a table, I will feel there was a boundary: My arm hit the table and it hurts. If I pay attention, I might perceive the table earlier and I won't get hurt. I can touch the table, but the boundary is not so relevant. Depending on what I focus on, I can notice the whole or something that separates and has boundaries. Likewise, I can notice the whole body or I can focus on the arm and say „ok, this is the arm and it goes from here to here". Alternatively, I can focus on a whole upper body including the arm, hand, shoulder.

Pain helps create that focus in a very specific way. If I follow it, it helps me be present.

I experience the same with fear. When I manage to relax about the fact that I am afraid, I can pay attention to what I need in order to calm down or be safe. I can then leverage fear to sharpen my senses and have a defocused, but highly aware moment of listening with my whole body. Once I have done that, it will often be easier for me to find out what I need to do next – even if the next activity is just breathing, relaxing, or calling up a friend in order not to be alone with the fear.

The sensation of fear can ask me to just be there, to feel what I feel and then move on. Or it can ask me to take very concrete action, like making sure that I have enough money to feed and house myself. In this way, fear is quite an amazing skill for survival.

At any moment in time, I am a body. So every experience has a physical aspect to it. To me, this is where the combination of the mind and the body becomes relevant for the practice of everyday presence. When I can relax my physical default reaction and instead respond, fear can fuel my mind to think quicker, my muscles to run faster or just give me the courage to speak about my true experience of a situation.

ATTENTION and ENERGY

In general, it seems to me that being my body, digesting and making sense of the world requires attention and energy. Sometimes I can choose when and how to invest attention and energy, but I cannot necessarily choose **if** I want to deal with a feeling or challenge. I might be able to choose to either push something away, to make myself hard and fight, or I can choose to relax, to feel the fear and discomfort and breathe to gain energy for being in a complex, uncertain situation. But whether or not the challenge or feeling arises seems to be out of my scope.

When I decide to stand by my choice, fully, I feel present. I feel present, when all of me – my body, my choices, my action – is invested in the current activity (and that might be doing the dishes, having a difficult conversation or standing on stage for a performance). When no part of me is disturbed or suffering and trying to pull my attention towards another matter. When fear can be part of this moment as well as pain or anticipation – then I can be in contact with the world. Then I can both notice my own needs, wishes, and fears and act according to what I perceive around me. I can communicate with others, take responsibility for a change that is required or offer my help if needed.

Maybe this is the sensation, that sometimes is described as silence of the mind – a term which I have previously had trouble with. If I define **silence** as the absence of disturbing noise, it might fit. And then the absence of disturbing noise needs a clarification because it still isn't the absence of noise, but of the *disturbance*. And this, I found, is a conscious choice I can make. A decision as to which thoughts and other input to follow, believe, or give importance and which to let just be noise.

This is a choice with physical consequences, that happens all the time. Every day, all day long, when I want to focus and be present for something specific.

I have noticed that the more I practice making this choice, intentionally and physically, the more situations occur when I can notice being both very involved, possibly afraid and *still* experience background noise – which then means that I need to choose continuously where to prioritize my attention and focus. If I start questioning whether I am **enough** in the moment... that is a version of actually leaving the situation and instead going to this meta-level of judgment. Any practice to strengthen Everyday Presence can be directed at one of these elements of the body (mind, pain and fear or attention and energy). Or combining several of them at once.

In the end, it is essential to me, that **attention to the body is about being able to interact with the world**, rather than to pull myself away from it.

Living as a (playful) Movement Discipline

As I perceive the world, everything that is alive moves. The movement may be ever so subtle, but there is movement in anything that is alive.

I would also sign a paper stating that everything changes. Even things of which I don't know whether or not they're alive, do change. Wear and tear are a kind of change or movement, just as the growth of a muscle is. The difference is: Whatever is alive is trying to live on, is trying to continue living and adapting to the conditions that change, maybe fixing or healing something that has been torn and finding a way to deal in a better, easier, simpler way with the challenges that inevitably seem to be there.

Every movement seems to somehow serve this purpose: **Living on**, adapting in an attempt to live better, with less resistance, less pain, less struggle and **more pleasure**.

Over the past years, I have come to see living more and more as a discipline of movement. The more playfully I practice this discipline, the smoother it feels and the easier it becomes to stay present.

What I mean by disciplines of movement: Any activity that focuses on movements that can be trained, isolated, specialized as well as improvised and played with (such as dance, martial arts, sports, playing a musical instrument etc.).

All these movement disciplines are of course part of the larger context of living. But also when comparing them at another level, living and movement disciplines have a lot in common: They involve me as a whole being, particularly the body, and any of these activities can either appear as a spontaneous activity that happens inspired by the situation or out of a preconceived idea to be trained and then performed. And they can be developed to be an intentional way of moving – for pleasure, for defense, to gain fame, to train specific skills etc.

In all these disciplines, it is common to learn and practice basic skills

in order to become accurate and flexible in the use of technique as well as for achieving more personal freedom within the set framework. Like which step to take when. Practicing which position of the arms might have an effect on how well I can adapt my strength and ability to connect. Noticing and adapting to the fact that balance will be influenced by my footwear, the position of my feet and in which direction my knees are turned – and so on.

TRAINING

I have been training different physical skills like playing the cello, playing volleyball, touch typing, dancing, from when I was a kid – and I have for the most part enjoyed the different practices. It was clear that to be a good dancer for example, it requires a good deal of training and dedication. And while one might or might not be talented, training, focus and regular practice do make a difference to the point of departure.

Looking at living as a similar practice of movement changed my experience of everyday life profoundly and represents a basis for the Everyday Presence that I am looking for. Previously, I was looking at living (less consciously but nevertheless) more like something that just happens coincidentally, while I was more or less **guilty for** or **a victim of** my circumstances. Noticing the movement discipline of living and its possibilities for the training of separate moves or certain combinations and playing with them, has been very empowering and is continuing to increase my freedom. Examples of the moves of life might be **biking without pain in the neck** or relaxing in a social situation.

Noticing that I can train almost any aspect or interaction I encounter, made a big change. I discovered the maybe obvious, but none-the-less impactful fact that anything in my life is in some way or another connected to a position and movement of my body. I can improve over time, becoming better at mastering a move or skill, and while sometimes this process is accompanied by frustration, I also experience success while moving between training special skills or basic ones over again.

My daily bicycle rides through Copenhagen are a simple example. They have become much smoother since I began paying attention to the way I hold my arms and shoulders in combination with the tension I'm holding in my neck. For a while, on every trip I made, I tried to relax my neck some more, eventually increasing my range of motion during the bike ride and reducing the soreness in my neck in general. As I went on, I also tried to increase attention to my general posture on the bike, noticing that I need much less force in my upper arms than I automatically used. Now I can actually relax more or less in the arms while cycling, and only tense up when I need to break or there is an unforeseen interruption on the path. That way, an everyday activity like transportation through the city became an activity that I can be movement-nerdy about and play with – eventually ending up biking with my hands completely off the handles. And without any soreness.

Similarly to my experiences in common movement practices, there was no preset amount of time telling me when I was going to be done. I would find out by playing again and noticing whether I was satisfied or not. **A move is smooth when it is smooth**. Not after five hours of daily training for five weeks.

I also practiced relaxing more in social situations where I felt awkward, and where afterwards I would notice that my belly was hard and tense.

First of all I began paying attention to my default posture when finding myself in this situation: pulling in the lower part of my belly, contracting the butt-cheeks, pressing the thighs together a little bit, holding my teeth slightly off center and lacking sensation for my feet. Then I tried to see what happens if I reduced the unnecessary effort. I didn't *need* to keep my jaw pushed to one side like that, relaxing the butt gave me more sensation in the feet and neither would even be noticed by the people around me, but it would give me a **much more relaxed experience of the situation**.

Each skill can be trained this way, whether it is gaining strength for being able to move others more easily, or gaining smoothness in an argument. From sitting effortlessly to running to the bus without asthma or hurting ankles to listening to the painful story of a client – when a situation is challenging me and I can't be in it as smoothly as I would like, I can look at the movement aspect of it and train until I'm satisfied.

As with a dance move that might get rusty if I haven't practiced in a while, or if I have merely been focused on something else, any of my skills can also get rusty. And as with anything that lives and evolves in such a complex manner, I might need to isolate certain movements to train them first in order to be more clear and precise about what I want to change, and then set them into a sequence. Then I train to do them without thinking about the movement as such but rather focus on the world around me and my impact on it, in order to evaluate whether my training did have the intended effect or what else the result will be.

Picking up on the bicycling example from before, that would mean that I now bike without thinking about the specific areas of my body and the individual movements that are involved most of the time. Instead, I notice the overall shifting of my weight, the wind, how much traffic there is around me and I experiment with bigger phrases like turning a corner with more precision, even without the hands on the handlebars.

IMPROVISATION and REPETITION

Besides the element of training technique and isolating specific movements, I also experience that similarly to other movement disciplines, in life as movement there is an element of improvisation, play and artistic expression that is not a technical skill in the same way. Yet it can still be trained and integrated into my practice for more freedom in interaction and movement.

In terms of living attentively, this is relevant because no situation will ever be **as practiced**. I can train to expand my chest and ribcage and relax my tongue more while I'm speaking, in order to have a stronger voice. I can train in many different situations, – relaxed, tense, upside down, while running – and still, the moment I'm standing in front of someone and I'm talking about an emotionally touching subject, everything will feel different than before. Now, if I have only trained one specific technique of expanding my ribcage, I might still get stuck with my voice, because there are other elements that influence my interaction. Being able to **improvise and focus on the intention** behind what I have trained – being able to express myself freely – thus allows me to move and interact more freely.

When I approach a challenging situation with this attitude of **practicing presence in a playful movement discipline**, any moment can become a training-ground for improvisation and freedom of movement. And I experience that applying this approach to something as unromantic as sitting at a conference, doing the dishes, riding my bicycle, having an argument or leading a decision-making process with others, has created a drastic change in my ability to enjoy and be well in challenging times. It adds an element of curiosity and takes the situation into a bigger context (that of learning more about moving freely), taking some of the pressure off the situation somehow.

While it might be clear that improvisation is an essential part of being able to... well... improvise in moments that seem a bit stuck, the fact that I can train a move or set of movements as technical skills to an everyday kind of challenge, is just such a relief. To me, it takes away the pressure of psychosomatic explanations or almost moralistic atmospheres around symptoms or limitations. And it lets the challenge and needed acts for change be very tangible and connected to the present moment instead of to the past.

And as any other movement discipline, it actually has this strong element of practice to it.

Coming from improvisation theatre and an attitude of **changing habits as much as possible**, in the beginning of developing and exploring this appreciation of practice, I met my own resistance to repetition. I often felt it to be an empty copy of the previous time.

During my somatic bodywork qualification training, one exercise in particular expanded my view on repetition. The instructions for this exercise were to take 15 minutes standing in front of a partner, connecting the hands, and both people were to push as strongly as possible without leaning (thus keeping the axis over their own feet) for the whole 15 minutes.

This was both physically and mentally challenging, and the instruction was to do it every day for three months. It wasn't an exercise that was simply done. It required an actual decision and commitment every day, as I also needed to find someone to agree to take on these challenging 15 minutes with me every day. Going through with this over the whole three months was an experience of learning about **determination**, committing to my own decision – no matter what happens – and about *repetition*.

I thought about the subject of repetition a lot, since the instructions for the exercise were the same over the whole period of time. However, just as the rest of my life was different every day – different time schedules, different personal state, different playing partners – following the same instructions lead to different experiences every day. After a while, I started to really like the exercise that I was dreading in the beginning. And after observing how the experience changed already during the first two weeks, I became more and more curious to notice how it would develop over the whole period. How could I stay present during this exercise and explore the experience, not in comparison to yesterday but as just coming from *right now*? This was powerful, and it changed my rejecting view of repetition into looking at it a bit more differentiated.

While before, repetition often seemed boring and annoying to me, I now experienced something that may be seen as obvious and basic knowledge: In order to learn to master something, I do need to repeat the movements and acts connected to it. I need it to become comfortable with one skill, build a base and then go on to the next thing. During this period of training, and actually paying attention to the different kinds of repetition since then, I have come to believe that actual growth and learning happen through attention – be that out of curiosity, pleasure, excitement, necessity or striving to be precise. In that case, the repetition isn't empty. And I guess this is why I would call it **a practice** or a training, as opposed to boring repetition.

I still dislike the thought of repeating something just because **this is** how we always do it. It seems lazy, boring or authoritarian and also lacking the **energy of creation**. Or doing something in the way that someone else used to do it – for me it lacks the energy of movement and growth, the aspect of my own thoughts and personality. And then I don't trust repetitions to be heartfelt. I don't see the point. „Because it's a tradition" gives me a sensation of being in a play instead of in my own life. It creates a weird distance to *now*.

However, when I use the trigger of repetition to be attentive in my practice of playful movement – and ask myself what this is really about, what is the heart of this repetition – it allows me to go beyond what I did the last time. I can then reduce the distance to the exercise and instead explore more curiously.

I experience this in any in any kind of movement practice, too. A purposeful movement, with attention and curiosity, can connect me to reality and make me awake, move me beyond what I did before. Without attention and energy, it'll be merely a mechanical repetition, potentially hurting me over time by excessive use of certain areas and under-stimulation of others. But with those qualities, I create diversity, even within a practice where I do the **same** exercise over and over.

I don't mind doing something that I've done before, as long as the motivation lies in the present. And that motivation *can* be to get better at a certain skill, opening my eyes to more detail in a similar environment and in this way expanding my horizon and experience of the moment. An example that is less obviously from the field of movement and more on the scale of living: If I travel to a place from my childhood and eat the same food, I can enjoy the nostalgia and try if it is as tasty as I remember. Or I can focus my attention on details within the surroundings that might have been less obvious in the previous experience. In this way, **I enrich my Now**.

When I learn a new dance or another form of movement, I enjoy learning from a teacher from time to time. Also in this aspect, Living is close to these disciplines of movement. I love to learn new tricks and hacks to make my living smoother. Sometimes by just watching and copying someone I admire. Sometimes by going to more formal learning environments and learning new skills and tricks from someone who explicitly teaches.

Over time, I have become increasingly picky with teachers, or rather more conscious in choosing which kinds of lessons I take from which teachers. The essence of a good dance teacher for me is someone who isn't trying to make me a copy of themselves, but one who gives me inspiration and shares their experience in how they trained, how they got to where they are and what they pay attention to in their dancing. They show me a move, **I try it**. Or I bring a move that I would like to know how to do and am struggling with. They show me where I do something that hinders me in making the move work. I try. And I decide if this is a move I want to be able to do and train after class or not. They're teaching me how I can get better at dancing from their experience of **learning to become a better dancer**.

They aren't offering me remedies that will *instantly* make me a dancer or shortcuts that work if only I understand or *believe* them. It is also clear that there isn't one right way, but that a lot of what it looks like in the end is personal taste.

The more I go for living more smoothly to practice Everyday Presence, the more I look for something similar in any teacher. An openness to share their knowledge, experience, and willingness to mirror what they perceive of me. Sometimes I want to learn a move; sometimes it's how I carry one very specific area of my body in a specific kind of interaction.

In dance, of course, it is very concrete and physical and it makes sense that, if I want to become better, I will need to practice. But now I also apply this approach when I learn anything from conflict resolution to cooking better jams...

The more I train, the more intuitive, the more natural the movements become to me – it is as simple as that.

And not necessarily training home alone with my mirror and myself. No – out and about! On the social dance floor, with other people around, is the best training ground! As I explored earlier, I also need to train the **improvisation in the Now**, the unexpected moments and unprotected conversations. Sometimes it goes fast and is fun, sometimes it is frustratingly slow, sometimes I'm suddenly able to do something and have no idea how.

In dancing, I noticed that sometimes even if I train a move over and over and over, somehow I don't get better at it. When I let it rest (or ignore it out of frustration) and then return to it after a couple of weeks, suddenly it's there. It's as smooth or as energetic as I was hoping. Probably there is a very good and solid scientific explanation for why that is and what is happening in the brain and body. For my everyday experience, my own observation and the possibility of noticing and applying this tendency to other aspects of living is more relevant though. Like in any other movement discipline, sometimes, in order to arrive at a place with more freedom of movement and inspiration for inventing new moves, the next step is to actually take a break.

To pause.

I'm not always sure what this means, though.

I notice that for me it is rarely the famous doing nothing (I never really found out what that actually is), but rather doing something else. Sometimes, a pause can be **moving the focus away from the intentional learning without letting go of the general intention of learning**.

Sometimes, of course, a pause means resting, sleeping, eating or taking a walk, moving without a specific intended outcome.

Maybe **doing nothing** is just that: Time spent without working towards a specific outcome? The time that sometimes is play, sometimes is sleep, sometimes is sitting in the sauna looking over the sea?

COMPLEXITY

Making art of any kind is complex. When I focus on all the little and big components that need to play together to finish a piece, a dance or a song, it is complex. And yet it is very simple – I just do it. And the next time I am working on something similar, I have the experience from before and I can use it to sharpen my perception of the new work or piece and discover details.

To me, it is the same in a larger context. Life and movement can be so incredibly complex. It isn't always just linear or obvious which movement I need to practice for being able to relax with the challenges I meet and for finding options in the current situation. Especially because I sometimes experience different and contradicting needs. Circumstances might pull me in different directions and thereby distort my movement. Not knowing which of the forces to refuse, which to agree to and where to put an emphasis, sometimes makes it confusing **where to start**.

As an example, I might wish to have more money in order to buy an apartment. If at the same time I also want to be independent and not ask for money, I need to figure out, which of those needs is more important to me. In order to do that and find a satisfying solution that allows me to stop worrying about the subject and move on, I will have to take more factors into account than just the immediate feeling, such as maybe my family's opinion and the situation of the city I live in. I may need to negotiate with different parties, myself etc. and move in between the different stages of decision making until I settle.

This complexity also means that I can start with any aspect that catches my attention. I can start by asking someone from my family. I can start with researching apartments or talking to the bank. Each **interaction will lead to a next move**, and the final result depends on them all together. If I approach this as a playful discipline of movement, I can focus on the physical experiences of the different aspects and my ways of being in them. I can basically start anywhere and try out what will happen to the rest of the *dance*. Whatever I do will have an effect, and then I will be able to see whether it brought me in the direction I was hoping for or showed me something new or unexpected. In the end I may find that moving apartment isn't my first priority right now, but it is actually a priority to find a way to earn more money. Or maybe independence isn't the most important aspect for me right now, whereas a place to live is.

Approaching the complexity of Living this way, I can enjoy the pleasures of the movement and even subjects that can otherwise be intense or heavy, gain a playful element in dealing with them.

BASIC PRACTICES

As I have learned in the past, I'm sure I will continue to learn new things and experience situations in new ways as I do. I will experience new versions of presence or distance, new versions of involvement and gaining energy. New versions of losing a sense of where I am, and finding it again.

For now, my exploration has led me to identifying the practices described in the following chapters as part of practicing and being able to choose Everyday Presence.

To know that I can practice is an empowering experience.

It means I have the key to my own development and am not merely dependent on my circumstances, genes and time passing. It allows me to participate in the course of my life.

Coming back to life being movement and adding the element of practice, this gives me the opportunity to practice the movements life consists of – if I so wish. Not only can I practice dedicated movement or artistic disciplines, or subjects that you can study in schools and courses. I can practice being well, having personal conversations, having light conversations, moving more smoothly through my life, when I decide to.

When I manage to be awake and actually **practice with a sense of commitment**, I experience lightness, pleasure and opportunity to enjoy. And in challenging moments it is easier to find a way to keep going and practice until another moment of lightness or peace arises.

I realize that part of the magic is the actual practice rather than the results. Part of this magic is also that it is not possible to arrive at a *finished* state. If I don't focus on them for a while, I become less elaborate or precise in the individual skill. The more committed my practice, the more detail I can find and explore, keeping the experience interesting and expansive at the same time.

For me, to keep an awareness of these practices is a choice that I can make every day. Sometimes one of them might have a higher priority than another. Sometimes I approach a specific challenge or subject with a focus on a specific one of the practices.

I realized that in any kind of regular practice, I need motivation. I need a reason to train or play around with them. Motivation can be intrinsic, just because I'm interested or curious, based on pleasure. Other times it comes from wanting or needing a specific outcome, like when I learned to deal with a budget for my business. That wasn't one of my intrinsic interests, but I wanted to be financially stable in order to able to relax, and I noticed that this could help me. The wish for stability was the motivation and driving force to learn these budgeting skills, and to get around my resistance to it, employing several of these practices was helpful.

In general, the basic practices are available to me as tools to be awake, to be present in moments that might be boring or challenging or to stay present at times that are thrilling and exciting.

They allow me to stay connected to reality through the body, to sharpen my ability to pay attention to the world around me and to practice Everyday Presence and enjoy life.

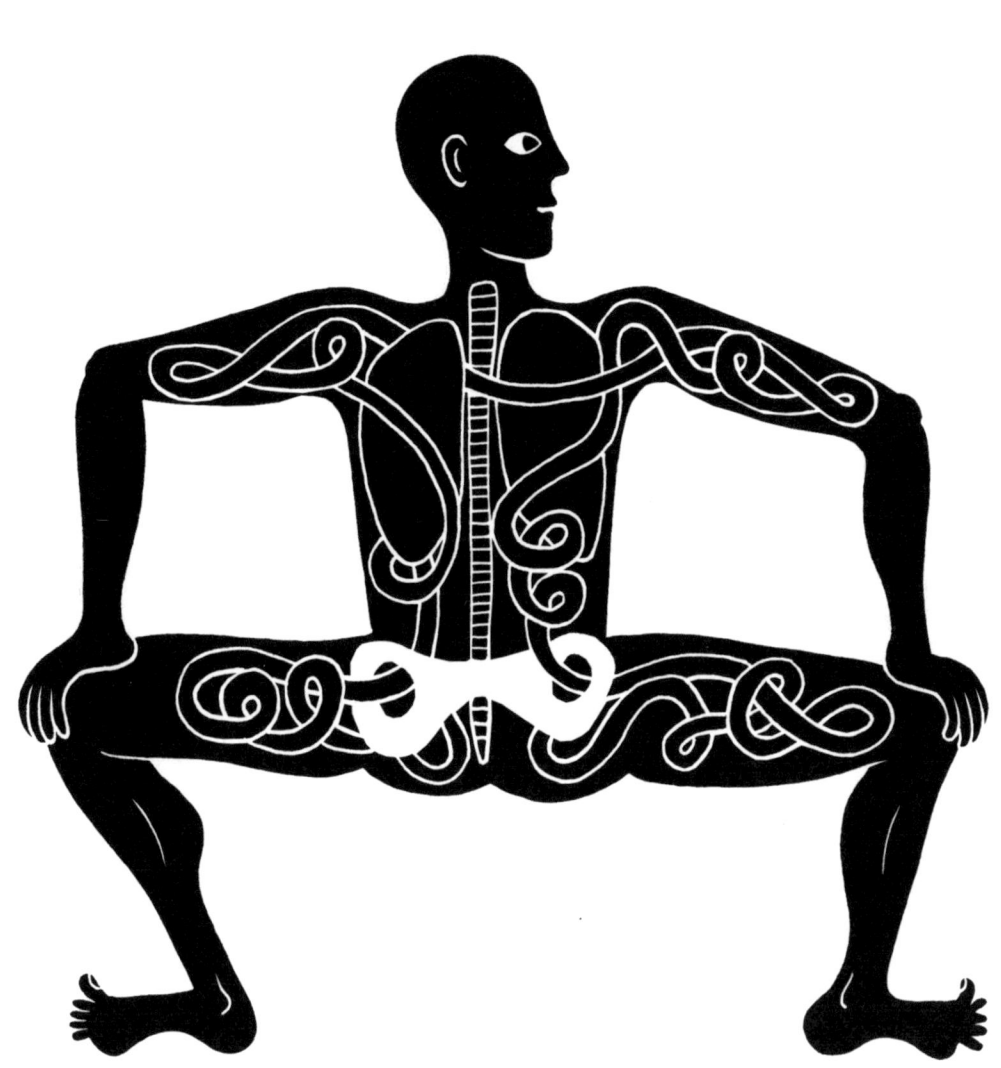

Accumulating and Releasing Energy

I wanted to find a no nonsense way of defining the term energy to fit my very concrete, physical experience of it without becoming too detailed – a really practical, usable definition. I want to start at a very profane place, and then elaborate with my own definition: „Energy is a property of objects which can be transferred to other objects or converted into different forms but never created or destroyed." (Wikipedia, January 2017)

It is an interesting term that is being used and interpreted in so many different ways. Especially in the self-awareness, body stuff, change-your-life-to-what-you-want-world some of the interpretations are quite spiritual and metaphysical – so vague – that I get dizzy just from hearing them. But I still use the term **energy**, because it is the only one that makes sense to me, talking about the aspect of living, I want to describe:

I mean energy as in heat and movement.

Energy as in the sensation of **having the capacity to do the task at hand**.

Being able to listen or to **concentrate**, to take a long hike, to dance at high speed or to listen closely.

Even when someone enters the room or touches me, I can experience energy as simply as **heat and movement** that affect me as a whole being. The wikipedia-definition applies here: Someone enters the room and adds their potential for creating change to what was already there. Others in the room of course can notice that.

That much about the base.

Energy.

I have always enjoyed living quite intensely, with many projects going on at the same time: Intense connections with friends, clients, partners, lots of movement and travels. Or – my life has always been quite intense, and most of the time I enjoy it. I don't think that is special, I just experience it as involving a lot of energy.
I know many people who live intensely, with similar waves of highs and lows or strong feelings as I have experienced. And while intensity can sometimes be overwhelming, I usually enjoy the boost and pleasure that comes from it, the power to create changes and move something in me or in the world around me.

I had to learn to **accumulate and maintain** the energy I need, in order not to disappear into the exhilaration or excitement and collapse after a while. In order to stay present, even when many things are going on. In order to notice, what I would need in the long run, not to burn out but to be able to stay in contact with other people and build sustainable strength. Learning to transform energy also allows me to stay present in times when there is less of the obvious, external intensity and I actually have a moment of calm or rest, as it makes me independent from external intensity or drama creating it.

I had heard and learned many times that I need to rest to have energy. That I need to slow down every once in a while. That I need to take a deep breath when it gets intense, in order to calm myself down. I heard, that I need to calm myself or reduce the input I get. Or that I need to say no, to prioritize, to have days when I do nothing.

While all of these actions and qualities I just mentioned became something I wanted to learn, they were not what I needed to begin with. At first thinking of this just made me desperate and like I had to want and wish less or reduce my own motivational power and drive.

It made such a difference to learn to increase the level of energy. To **accumulate the** energy I need. I can now deal with and adjust to the level of intensity I like, *as well as* I can focus on reducing the intensity. I noticed that I can use my drive and this wanting; make more of it and create a situation for myself, where I don't run over my body with my dreams and ideas.

The first tool I learned in this quest to gain energy was to use breathing as a tool that gives me energy rather than *just* calms me down.

So simple.

So cheap.

So priceless.

Learning to notice and practice different versions of breathing changed not only my experienced energy level but changed a lot of symptoms, too. When I used to have a headache, it could've knocked me out for more than a day, suffering. Today it is often enough to take ten minutes focusing on my breathing, playing with different tempo, sounds, directions and movements. And then the headache is either gone or at least I have a clearer sensation of what I need to do next in order to **stop suffering**. I might notice that I need to eat, that I need to move more or stretch. Or sometimes I just need to change the subject or activity I'm busy with.

I **practice breathing** in different ways and am paying attention to it **daily**. One way could be noticing the rhythm of my breath and trying different speeds, another could be paying attention to an area in my body that is involved in the movement of breathing. Or just making sure that I actually do breathe during any activity.

And I also do specific breathing exercises from time to time. I experience the moment of attention to what happens in my body while and after I breathe in a specific way, to be an important part of actually creating a sustainable supply of energy for myself with such exercises. It gives a moment to practice relaxing with the sensation of flow or warmth that is created. Noticing which areas of my body are activated and which are still sleeping; and relaxing with the sensation in the head that changes during this kind of exercises.

I also use everyday activities and **a moment of attention to my breathing at random times** as training during the day. Both in order to just have more variety in my possibilities for breathing and to adapt what I had trained to the current situation.

Right now I am still alive, which means I sometimes have pain and I experience situations that become intense. But I have much more control over my breathing now and can adapt it to the situation I am in, providing an opportunity for the body to create the energy needed.

> *I learned that I can breathe when I'm cold to raise my body temperature.*
>
> *I learned, that I can breathe in a way that brings more flow to the head which allows me to think more clearly.*
>
> *I learned that I can breathe in a way, that just allows me to create a subtle movement in my body, in situations that otherwise feel stuck.*
>
> *I learned that I can breathe in order to not fall asleep in situations where I want to stay awake.*

I learned that I can use the rhythm of my breathing to anker my focus when the dance is becoming fast and I just want to continue to follow my partner and not get out of breath...

The list goes on.

I have been asked several times how exactly I breathe in these situations, and I hesitate to write about it. Mostly because it is such a physical experience, but also because there is not *one specific way* for me. Rather, it feels like the **variety makes the difference**. I have trained breathing fast, long, slow, with different areas of the body in focus... And I have had the experience of influencing my body in this way, so if one version of breathing doesn't work at that specific moment, I play with this approach and experiment with different forms while still trying to relax.

Today I don't get as exhausted as I used to be on a quite regular basis. And when I'm exhausted, I'm not devastated or disappointed anymore, and I recover more easily. Instead of suffering and waiting to be *back up and with drive*, I use some of my time to play or do unimportant and fun things – like watching a nice movie or baking cakes – until I want to do something else again.

Another important aspect to maintaining a higher level of energy has been considering and **giving importance to the basic physical needs** of the previously described material component of my body. Taking this into consideration in situations where I'm emotionally challenged in some way (I feel overwhelmed or sad or angry, sometimes without knowing what it is about), helps me take away a lot of the drama of those feelings.

Instead of being all overwhelmed, filling up my thoughts with the search for reasons and questioning my whole life and all of my decisions, I have learned to notice feelings as signs of needing to take care of my basic needs as well. Just like a physical sensation of hunger or thirst, an emotional sensation can be a sign for me to pay attention whether I might need to eat or move or sleep, in order to have enough energy. Without the physical basis, there is nothing to transform...

Part of this practice was to learn to acknowledge those basic needs as **needs** and as **basic** to begin with. While it should probably be obvious that taking care of sleep, food, movement and digestion etc. is relevant to maintain a high level of energy, it still took some practicing for me. Eating and having to go to the toilet used to be so annoying and in the way of me doing **my thing**. Making sure that I eat well is still the more challenging of the basic needs for me to practice and incorporate into my day. It still hasn't become natural to just do, but I remind myself to eat during a day filled with interesting and exciting things. I practice to not only eat, but to eat cooked food that feels good in my belly. Bonus: When I do feed myself in a satisfying way, I get all excited about that fact. (I still really love it when someone else cooks for me, though. Very much.)

The food issue also works the other way around: Feeling hungry or tired can actually lead me to a sadness or another feeling that is occupying part of my attention. When I know that I have eaten or slept, i.e. have taken care of the basic needs, it is easier for me to interpret a feeling of hunger or fatigue as a trigger to notice which feeling or thought needs attention. I might not need to eat or sleep, but instead to actually deal with discomfort. The feeling is not less valid, but I might just need to cry or breathe or talk with someone in order to go on, rather than sleep or eat.

I used to think that I have to sleep when I am tired. And I was very good at going to sleep when I was tired. Now, I can first check what breathing might do, or movement. Then, if I'm still tired, I sleep. Also, sometimes I'm not interested in being highly energetic, and I actually look forward to the coziness of sleeping. So I do that. I just allow my body to get the **time to rest** that I apparently need.

For me, it made a difference to stop sleeping a specific amount of time. Instead of the average number of hours, I started to pay attention to whether or not I'm tired and then sleep accordingly.

Again: So simple, so **priceless**.

There are nights when I sleep five hours and feel full of energy. There are other nights when twelve hours seem to be just right. Sleeping the same amount of time every night over a longer period of time doesn't really do it for me. Adapting to my perceived energy level does.

I look at all of these ways of dealing with basic needs as ways of generating energy to maintain myself both in times of intensity as well as times of boredom. This enables me to be in touch with the world and people without getting grumpy, overwhelmed or extremely tired, thus building a base for being more present.

When I do this on a regular basis, I also notice much clearer when I get sick. The days when I can't just breathe more and then all is good. Where I actually do feel so exhausted that I need to lie for a day or two, go see a doctor or whatever. Those days stick out so much more now. And then it is easier for me to take the time to rest and recover, knowing that I need exactly that.

Something to play with: Attention to Breathing

https://soundcloud.com/ninia-schwan/exercize-attentiontobreathing

Honest Description to deal with Discomfort

This practice is very much about an attitude, I guess. I aim to be ruthless and honest about what I perceive – both concerning what I do, think or feel *and* what happens with the people around me.

Honesty towards myself means that I need to swallow my pride and notice what is really going on.

Honesty to share an experience with someone else, means that I will make myself vulnerable. And it is always my choice whether I want and need to integrate this step, or if it would actually be enough to honestly describe a moment to myself in order to create a change or be in it with more presence. Either way it can be challenging, because it isn't always comfortable to realize unflattering things for myself either.

I had a strong experience of this related to body image recently.

Everyday Presence to me is very much about noticing the situation with the whole body, and not in fact observing the body from *the outside*, or trying to hide a part of it and putting effort into that. Now, for a while, the size and sensation of my belly was disturbing me. And I didn't want to admit that to myself. I work with people all day long, I find every body I meet interesting as it is. Also when I see them dance, I'm more interested in how each body moves with its particular shape than to see only perfectly proportioned bodies dance. I find it distracting when someone is wearing clothes that are too small or that **mold** their body into a certain shape, simultaneously limiting their freedom of movement. Or when I see someone holding their body contracted in a way *to try to hide* something that remains visible – only now contracted. I was very convinced that body image wasn't a relevant subject for myself to look at, because anyway, I'm not trying to look perfect.

However... As I was at a dance event, feeling slightly off and unable to be fully present and focused on my dances, I realized that I was busy with my belly, keeping it tight and holding it in. This was the first **uncomfortable discovery**: I'm not immune to body shame. As I decided to relax my belly more and be honest about my body, breathing and relaxing through this moment of shame – the second thing that I realized was, that I wasn't so busy with whether or not my body looks beautiful, but rather whether I appear to be healthy and balanced within myself. And apparently I had had an idea that a less than flat belly is a sign of imbalance. Rather a visible sign of some kind of psychosomatic problem that I didn't dare to look at or didn't manage to take care of.

I was surprised by this twist – feeling the same shame as proposed by beauty magazines, whose arguments I don't buy, but instead applying the arguments of the somatic movement that I'm in.

Discovering this twist in my own perception was uncomfortable. But discovering this argumentation also allowed me to deal with it more directly. First of all, in that moment of realization, I was able to physically relax my belly, and the next couple of dances were much more pleasurable. I focused on integrating the sensation of my belly into the dance instead of hiding and contracting it, and finding new movements and sensations in the dance. This was fun, as it gave me new inspiration for improvisation.

The belly was still a bigger part of my experience than I would have liked for being fully present in that evening. But instead of limiting the joy of my dancing, I actually learned something new and it was amusing. (And about the shame; most probably no one else beside myself noticed a change in the shape of my body. They were all just enjoying their evening of dancing – and anyone busy with judging other people's shapes to such detail in a place like that would probably be unpleasant to be around no matter what.)

There was a third element of learning in that experience: As I relaxed my belly more, I noticed that a pain I sometimes have in the right side of my lower back, reduced and the area became more flexible and alive. So I actually became curious to learn more about this and possibly not only increase the pleasure of my dancing, but also the sensation afterwards, having less pain or stiffness in the lower back.

Like this episode, there are many moments of slight insecurity or even very clear feelings of disagreeing with something or someone throughout the day and life.

Moments when it can be tempting to hope, to pretend, or to ignore what I actually perceive in order not to experience the discomfort arising from it.

Moments when it would be so much nicer to tell myself a story that makes my painful, inattentive act towards a friend a little bit nicer because I didn't mean it.

Or the other way around, when I tell myself that it probably isn't true, that this person I see is abusing their position to tell people what to do, instead of actually letting them decide. I can tell myself „It's probably just me", or be confused and unsure to avoid noticing what is actually going on.

It is more painful to notice both sides – that possibly I had a good reason for what I did. But also, I really, really hurt my friend in a way that wasn't necessary. And in the other case, that that person might have done many amazing things, but also they're abusing their position of power... It is more painful and more uncomfortable, because it doesn't provide an easy solution for what to do next.

In vulnerable moments, practicing honest description can intensify a feeling – it can give a sensation of being alone or exposed (even if no one else notices it), especially if I am aware of something that no one else mentions or that seems to be taboo.

The practice in this for me is to describe honestly **and physically, when I experience a discomfort** that I want to be able to move on with.

I am very good at describing things that I'm unhappy about, in a way that is constructive or diplomatic. I used to be very good at shutting up when I disagreed with someone and didn't feel like going into a discussion – and then just doing what **I wanted to be doing** anyway. But I also realized at some point, that a part of this skill is also being very good at lying. White lies maybe, but still lying. Saying I'm excited when I'm scared but don't want to show vulnerability could be one example. Or as in the example above, believing that I don't have an issue with body image and shame, as I don't buy into the perfect body form of visual beauty-mantra.

A lie, of course, can also just be a version of the truth that leaves out parts that might be more uncomfortable. Like slightly twisting the expression of my actual intention when I the discomfort of being honest is stronger than the discomfort of being polite. I think it is a great skill to be able to use in situations where being polite is important for some reason. Because being honest about disagreement or vulnerability isn't necessarily relevant in every situation.

Over the past years, I noticed that this diplomacy, if it is not a conscious choice but applied out of a habit, could also be a way of preventing me from actually being present in the moment. It adds a filter to my expression, not only towards the outside but also towards myself, and it can make it more challenging to notice what I really mean, feel or think, when I use it automatically. I also realized that even if there might be this element of discomfort, the **connections I have with people, feel more real when I'm being honest**. They are more direct and often the results of these interactions are more creative or tailored to those involved.

Some people have let me know that it can seem harsh or mean when I'm honest about what I perceive, but I don't actually think it

BASIC PRACTICES

is. To me, there is a difference between being honest about what I perceive and how I evaluate what I perceive. I can still notice that I didn't mean to hurt my friend and that I actually love her even when I admit that I was stupid and ignorant and hurt her in a way that was unnecessary.

To me it becomes a more real experience, more credible, when I'm honest about the different levels of the interaction. Plus, I can learn from this experience to be more attentive if a similar situation should arise again and I want to act differently than I did last time. Furthermore, I still have a **choice how to express** what I have perceived. I can still choose to notice and evaluate how much of my perception it is relevant to share with my environment, and how much of it is actually only about me.

For example, if I find myself in a situation where I notice that a person presenting a subject is insecure, I can choose whether or not it is relevant for the moment to share this observation. It might actually be that voicing my observation would only be about me showing off that I perceived something vulnerable – and actually shaming the person even more. On the other hand, if that person in their insecurity is claiming to talk about facts while leaving out relevant information, asking them about the insecurity might improve the experience for the other people present.

In my experience discomfort comes in different shapes – often connected to feelings or sensations that for some reason or another I have **decided** (or learned) are unwanted. It can be feeling shame, uncertainty, it can be feeling the other person's pain, it can be noticing someone else's jealousy over my success – or worse, my own jealousy over someone else's... (Worse as in *more shameful to admit*...) However, in order to be present, I realize **this is what I have to be with**. I don't always have to act on it, but I experience it as an essential part of being present to agree to noticing that it might be uncomfortable. I don't just want to stay present and awake when it is nice and cozy, but also in these moments.

This is why I need to be able to raise and maintain my level of energy, too. I need to be able to distinguish between a discomfort that is harmless and temporary and one that might need extra attention or to be stopped. Staying in pain that doesn't change, or just describing honestly how someone hurts me without stopping them or going to the doctor is not what I am aiming for, although it has happened along the way.

Therefore intentionally raising my level of energy needs to be coupled with honesty: I need to realize honestly, when I cannot deal with the discomfort on my own, no matter how much energy I have. When it's not just something that I can be in and be curious about the next moment. When staying there is taking up all my resources, then I might need to ask for help.

So the practice is the movement between noticing and agreeing to uncomfortable sensations without immediately pulling away from them because of the discomfort they provoke, and then noticing the relevance for the current situation. My jealousy might be irrelevant in terms of action towards the person I'm jealous of – but it might show me something that I also want and am currently missing. When I accept to feel this, and detach it from that specific person and instead relate it to **my personal need**, I might find actions in the future that will lead me to achieving what I was longing for. And then jealousy can actually be a strong force to drive me, instead of being something destructive that I'm *not allowed* to feel.

Maybe one of the most frequent sensations that appear when I'm being honest in everyday life is that I have no idea what is going on.

If I think about it, I don't know why I feel a certain feeling or what would be the best thing to do next. But if I stay attentive to the experience, and listen, I usually find solutions or next steps that deal with what is happening, instead of fixing a superficial semi-problem with an immediate reaction. The first step for me is to honestly look at the moment myself. If it seems relevant, I also share my perception with those I'm sharing the moment with – whether I messed something up, or someone else did... Whether I am proud and happy or I am in doubt and want to explore a feeling.

Honesty and agreeing to notice discomfort is also very much connected to staying present with other people, to being there when they experience strong emotions or thoughts that might be unwanted. Staying there and seeing them clearly, containing their experience without going into an immediate solution based on my default reaction, often gives a strong sensation of presence as well. Taking the time to listen to their experience as well as honestly noticing my own in it, and how the two relate. **Does the other person need a hug, a slap, me to go away?** Staying and noticing, what happens when I experience this? Which questions arise?

Sometimes the discomfort just comes from the discrepancy between what I perceive and what is being said or acted out loud. Or the discrepancy between my experience of the situation and that of the others involved... Which might lead to a good conversation and exchange – or settling in having two different experiences.

In these situations I focus on **staying connected to my physical experience of the moment, to stay relaxed and with energy.** To stay connected with the truth of my experience as well as my environment – and then the excitement of the situation can actually give me more energy, or else I at least widen my horizon.

Exploring Isolation and Connection

In dancing, isolation means to isolate one part of the body and moving it while simultaneously keeping the rest of the body still. To train this, you have to learn to stop automatic connections that otherwise would be triggered, when you, for example, move the little finger. Instead you learn to control a specific muscle or group of muscles. At the same time, you train to relax the rest of the body. So actually, it is only partly an isolation. As it needs simultaneous attention and awareness to the whole body it is also an act of connection.

I found this in playing the cello as well as in training to be a better volleyball player. In order to improve the smoothness of the overall experience, I would take the time to train one specific move; one specific finger maybe, or how to take a step. I'd train it so many times that I could really pay attention to the little details of the movement. And then put it back into the whole movement pattern or just play – now with increased attention to integrating the practiced feature into the game.

Especially relaxing the areas that aren't actively involved in the activity I'm training is relevant when I want to save energy and be precise. In sports this is obvious: When I want to serve a ball and at the same time contract my left shoulder completely, my serve will be less precise and probably less powerful than it could be. Part of my energy is invested in the muscles of the left shoulder, and the tension there might pull my right arm towards the left instead of allowing a smooth, straight swing. A similar thing happens when I'm partner dancing. If I contract my upper belly while I'm dancing, I'm creating a tension that will most probably disturb the elasticity of my arms. I need the elasticity in my arms in order to really be able to communicate with my partner about where we're going. So, this tension not only takes energy and makes me stiffer, it also influences **my ability to communicate and connect** and will thus influence the quality of the dance for my partner, too. On the other hand, if I totally collapse in my diaphragm and my arms are floppy, I won't be able to communicate very clearly either. The energy that I need to create a fast turn or change of direction, will just disappear into the nowhere of collapsed muscles and bisect the joy of the dance.

I found that the same can also be true in other experiences, for example of connection with a partner. To improve the experience and the pleasure of a conversation or daily living together, I can thus train by looking at specific skills or areas of my body in relation to the rest. For a while, I can focus on creating enough power in my core and diaphragm to not collapse and rather keep elasticity in my whole body. And I can practice relaxing my arms and shoulders while I'm walking hand in hand, so that the information can go from my partner through my whole body and vice versa. Walking hand in hand might less obviously be an act of communication. Relaxing unnecessary tension, however, might **allow me to notice details** in the other person's mood through noticing their movement.

Sometimes this means that I will meet a sensation of fear or insecurity if I'm not contracting my upper belly in the same way I used to. Instead of contracting my belly to keep balance, I might need to breathe more and really pay attention to the ground under my feet to notice that I'm not actually falling, as I'm afraid of. Or I might need to say stop to a person if they're coming closer than I actually want them to. I can do this with words or with my action, but the important thing is that I notice things in a new way than before I started with the training.

I find Isolation to be one of the best things, to apply also to other, more everyday kind of activities, because I experience it as extremely **empowering**. When I notice that my attention in certain conversations is easily distracted while I would actually like to be more present there, I can learn to notice which change in my body allows me to do that. Often I discover, that something as simple as for example relaxing the jaw every once in a while, allows me to stay more focused and present when I'm listening to a subject that requires my concentration. This isolation then allows me to stay connected in the conversation.

As I'm curious about movements and physicality with this approach, I find that any activity can become a physical exercise and that I can make it into a practice. If I want to be able to connect more easily with the people I meet in the street, I can take the time to observe myself in interactions or ask someone I trust to help me out with their observation – not their judgment, mind you – of what they can see me do in this situation, whether I'm stiff somewhere or jumping over a sensation by contracting in an unnecessary way. After some time of observation, I can then try to experiment with one of those stiff or contracted areas of my body – how do my interactions change when I intentionally relax my butt? Or what happens when I relax my diaphragm and breathe with attention to expanding the chest while I speak to people I care for? Like I have learned to improve my skill of serving a volleyball straight by relaxing the other shoulder, I might be able to listen more attentively and speak more clearly when I relax my diaphragm and chest.

When I realize that I often end up with a headache after I have been in a conference for the whole day, I can have a look at several things. I can start by very physically noticing the position of my body and isolate the way I hold my head. I might become aware of a tension I'm holding in my neck in the process of focusing on the different people. When I isolate this area, I can experiment how much of the tension I actually need in order to hold my head, and how much I can relax. Considering that I'm sitting, I might not need to contract my thighs and knees or hold my lips tense.

I notice that I can direct my attention to this kind of local tension and that in itself will create a change. And if sitting in conferences is something I choose to do regularly, I can train explicitly and really just practice sitting, in order to then be able to relax more intuitively when I'm back at the conference and want to be able to use my energy on the content there, rather than irrelevant tension.

It could also be that, when relaxing the rest of my body and just holding the necessary tension to keep my head up, I realize that all the other tension wasn't from my sitting position but an attempt to keep me from exploding onto people who were dominating the meeting with unhelpful comments. Then finding a new way to deal with this frustration might be a result of my attempt to simply relax my neck, so **I have more options than either exploding or creating a headache**...

While in an explicit dance or movement discipline it is common to change a move or improve details, somehow in an everyday situation like this, these changes can feel scary. For some reason, how I sit in a meeting can feel more related to my identity than how I hit the ball – so changing something and isolating it into just a specific movement can feel as if threatening my identity. I think this is why these kinds of changes can sometimes be more challenging **in real life** than in a movement class. On the other hand, one of the reasons for training to become good at something like dancing or playing ball is the pleasure of overcoming previous limitations – be that a physical or emotional or mental conception of myself. This practice of isolation of movements and then focusing on the connection again afterward means that I could theoretically change anything and any habit I have. And overcome previous limitations in everyday life.

And yet, I can only change the things I have a motivation to change. I notice that just like I never got truly interested in horseback-riding – a very physical activity that can probably be very well compared to partner dancing – there are certain activities or habits in my life that I'm not interested in changing. And then there is no energy in it. The little nerd in me doesn't get excited to figure out, what would happen if I became an expert at knitting in a relaxed way. So I only knit very little, and when my fingers are tired, I stop.

Sometimes it does appear, though, the little nerd, and invites me to experiment with a new way of sitting on the bike, just for the sake of it. A new way of holding my hands when I meet a new person, just to try what kind of experience this will invite and in which way it might influence our dance.

I can also be intrigued to practice my attention and connection to the more generic qualities of a body part. Noticing how I can contract and relax a muscle for example. Noticing where my body is – where my foot is touching the surface, where the air is touching me and where there might be a piece of clothing.

What are the differences in these sensations?

How does it feel when I move my arm slowly up and down and what changes in me, when I do this faster?

Or with contracted hands?

What changes in my perception, when the sensation of my legs is very present?

What if I shift my weight, while I'm sitting?

And how does it relate to my ability to connect with the people next to me, my ability to be present in the subject we're talking about?

Something to play with: Contraction and Relaxation

https://soundcloud.com/ninia-schwan/exercise-contraction

Playing with Patterns

Something, that appears when practicing life, are patterns. Patterns and habits to me are very closely related. Many people talk about habits, even gladly so about bad habits, and the subject can easily turn into a discussion of right or wrong. However, approaching habits from a more neutral angle has been much more valuable for me. While I see a **pattern as a specific set of movements** (shapes, sounds or even thoughts) activated in the same order, a **habit is an automated pattern** that I more or less intentionally repeat after being triggered. A trigger can be external like being asked a question or also internal, like the decision for a specific morning meal. In this definition I am not imposing any moral judgment – whether or not I like a habit or pattern and whether I enjoy it or not, is a different conversation.

I used to have strong opinions about habits and was convinced that they needed to be broken. Mainly, I think, because I easily got bored. Changing location, habit, activity was exciting. I also hated being put into boxes and having to define my identity, which I felt I had to when describing my habits, what I do, or who I am. I easily dismissed doing something **just out of habit**, because it's what I'm used to or **out of an automatic pattern** as something to be avoided and harmful. It was as if I saw acting out of habit as morally less worthy than breaking a habit, changing it and doing something new. My arguments were, that doing something out of habit was the same as doing it *just* to be comfortable. Or acting according to a group's habit was not individual enough. I deemed acting out of habit as not conscious or creative enough. Today I am more relaxed about habits and see these reasons as descriptions rather than judgments of habitual behavior.

However, something I still find disturbing is when someone uses their habits as an excuse for doing something they don't want to be doing. They might say what to do, it's a habit, thus giving away their responsibility to an abstract entity of habits which they have no control over. Taking for granted that this is just as it is: **well, well.**

Using habit as this huge element of their being that could only be changed with unreasonably large amounts of effort.

When I use a more moral-neutral approach, I describe habits and patterns as the manifestation of a practice or repetition. In other words: They are a manifestation of one way of being and acting, that has become more familiar and comfortable, and where each step is determined by the previous one.

This in itself doesn't necessarily pose a problem. I see limitations, though, when these habits become my only option of acting or being, and when any alteration would **threaten** me or get me stuck. If I want to be present, I need to be open to the situation **developing in a way that I didn't expect**. This is why attention to habits becomes relevant in relation to Everyday Presence. When habits have the effect that I no longer realize the **wonder of what might happen next** to allow me to actually experience something new. Or when they just cut me off from the experience of connecting with the other people *and* needs around me in this moment. Then they limit my presence in everyday life.

One of my biggest motivations for learning to become more free of them and be able to play with habits and patterns, besides wanting to be more well myself, is when I notice that if I don't change, I'm hurting people I care about. Out of habit, out of pain and not knowing how to deal. I might have been just snapping at people, not seeing that they too are exhausted or totally exploiting their resources. Or I might have acted defensively and mean in order to protect myself. There have been moments when I was patronizing and others when I criticized others because I was in pain. All of this came out of a habit – an old pattern and reaction to fear.

One of my motivations to deal with fear and pain is that I believe, that people do crazy things out of old patterns of reaction to fear or pain, and that this hurts the world. In the daily news, we hear about more outrageous versions of this (wars, violence, neglect...), but I also find destructive reactional patterns to be a factor in my own everyday life.

One situation when I certainly wasn't playing with patterns but instead taking them very seriously, was around stereotyping jokes and comments. As long as I can remember, I have reacted quite strongly to them. I felt locked in and pressured when I thought I should be defining my identity – or other people's identity – through such a joke. I also get rather queasy when people start talking about their personality, and horoscopes freak me out as well as **national identities**. I was so allergic to these concepts that I neglected any kind of generalization and was very keen on **always** saying everything as openly and correctly as possible. Now, as you know, this is impossible and it can also be quite exhausting. How would I even think that I could ever take everything into consideration? I wouldn't be able to, but I was trying hard, and in this, I could be quite unforgiving and without humor. I judged people who did use stereotypes, to be insensitive, blind and maybe also dumb – thereby also putting myself above them with my pride.

In the past couple of years I have become more relaxed with this issue, realizing that my own reactions are patterns I can be aware of and play with. Personality types just as horoscopes can sometimes offer a structure for the mind to think within and be used as a model that needs to be discussed, adapted, changed etc. While I still get annoyed when someone is presenting such systems or is arguing using the systems as a point of reference as if they are the truth and not just models, I become less agitated today when someone makes a simple joke – and **I make stupid and simplifying jokes** myself. I enjoy them.

I would even say today, that I can often see which kind of culture someone grew up in or spends a lot of time in when I see them moving (especially freestyle party dance). I recognize that certain social cultures have stereotypical traits. I sometimes think **that's such a stereotypical male behavior** or so typical mother behavior. I am no longer offended when someone tells me that I'm acting very German, or that I move in a feminine way. Instead, I am more curious to learn which of my actions or movements are supporting this pattern that someone else might see. Or which of their habits makes them come to this conclusion. When I'm present, I can notice more than just the words of the joke and notice the atmosphere as well – and know whether what was stated was harmful or actually fine in the context. I also know that I am more than that image and don't feel like I have to fit into one pattern anymore, into that one mask. Instead, **I can pick it up or drop it**. I can slightly change it, trying to notice when the general impression will change, go all in and exaggerate, or just relax about the fact that of course I too move in patterns.

The more I learn to notice my body, the more quiet I perceive my mind in this regard. While a predefined category is fixated, the body is constantly changing – even if only in small things and even if there are also things that remain the same. The more I can just **be my body**, the more I can be in different contexts, mingle with different groups, meet all kinds of people, do different activities. I'm not dependent on a single activity or group to confirm my identity. When I'm confident within myself, changes in context don't question who I am; they just add another flavor, another aspect to my life. Then, someone else's category for me doesn't matter so much anymore. And I can start to play.

Being aware of habits and patterns and acknowledging that they are not the only way but simply the usual or preconceived way, gives me the freedom to play by ignoring them or challenging them in situations when they're not helping me. When I am aware of a habitual reaction and how it limits me, I can learn to notice when this pattern starts. For example when shutting up instead of disagreeing out loud when someone gets very angry and loud leads to the other person actually getting their way every time. When does the sequence start, what are the steps I know from myself that will follow? I close my mouth and my breathing becomes shallow. And how might I react differently? This awareness is one of the reasons why I enjoy learning to notice more and more of my body. I learn to notice more clearly when I am reacting out of habit and adapting to a social category, and when I act according to who I am right now –

BASIC PRACTICES

and where those two overlap. When am I following a pattern and when am I breaking it? And, of course, **what happens when I change any of the steps**, for example by physically opening my mouth and breathing more?

Sometimes I notice a habitual feeling, yet I don't quite know how to change anything about it. But I know that if it is bothering me, I can learn to deal with it. I can pay attention to **what happens in my body and play with alternatives**. Eventually, I might change my reaction or my attitude, or I might not. But all along, I can identify this as me.

Being able to play with patterns instead of feeling trapped by a habit, allows me to move much more freely among others. It gives me another tool for practicing Everyday Presence, as I have another aspect to pay attention to in moments when I would like to feel a stronger connection with the reality around me **right now**. Sometimes a new behavior might bring me closer. In other situations, being able to activate a specific behavior pattern and just following its rules might allow me to communicate more directly to a person that is very used to this way of doing things. I might be able to talk at a different level than if we need to negotiate the frame or format first.

With this awareness comes a freedom to play. **To go all in on a mask for a day**, for example. Or to choose which rules to follow and which not to include in my game, depending on the situation and the desired outcome of a situation.

Something to play with: Training with a Recurring Position

https://soundcloud.com/ninia-schwan/exercize-recurringposition

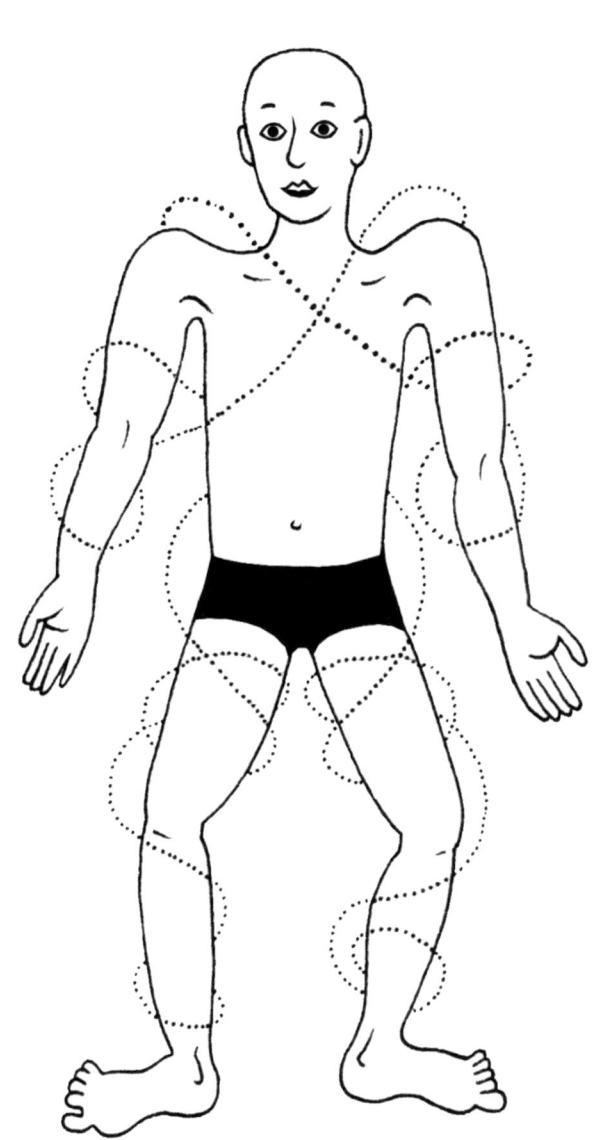

Listening with the Body

So, as I perceive it, my body is more than a vehicle to carry me around – it is a device for perception.

The practice of listening with the body is an intentional activity of *using* this device when I'm evaluating a situation, taking into consideration more of my physical experiences than just the sounds that I hear, the images I see, or facts that I know. I retrieve meaning from what I perceive with my whole body. That could be in a conversation, in the actual listening to another person. It could be in dealing with a random situation in the world, when I'm interpreting an event and its impact on me to find out what to do next. It could be after falling, checking how severely I'm hurt and what I *need* to take care of.

When I listen, as in holding the space for the conversation partner to unfold, I have the time to let more of the story be told before I draw conclusions from it. I am able to notice nuances that could get lost in a fast default reaction to any impuls or sensation. With the middle section of my body I might get a sensation that informs me about someone's need for me to move closer or further away in a conversation. While with my thoughts and ideas I might still be holding on to wanting to make a relationship work, my physical sensation can very clearly and non-judgmentally show me that I need to walk away from it in order to take care of myself and my general well-being. When I relax with these sensations, I have more of a choice whether to react fast right now, or whether to be passive. I can take a moment when I miss someone, for example, and double check with more of the story in my body to choose whether to contact them now and how – or not. Maybe I just want to feel this sensation of missing them and the memory of a love connected to it.

There are moments when I can easily interpret what a feeling or fear is about and in that case, listening like this helps me to take care of it. Other times it seems too complex for the moment and I just notice *fear*. Then I relax with the fact that I'm afraid (without having to defend or pretend or be proud). Using this approach, I often feel energetic – and I might be able to **invest this energy** in a subject that requires it at the moment.

For me, listening with the body is a very technical skill and at the same time some kind of magic. Like musicality in a dance – following structures and impulses that can be observed clearly, in combination with an element of surprise, mistakes and uncontrolled movements and intuitive perfection.

The first step to learning **listening with the whole body** was for me to not be disturbed by the regular processes of my body. Besides agreeing that they are processes that keep me alive, I also need to not be distracted by them when I want to listen with the body to what is happening now. I needed to not be disturbed by the sound of my breathing. Not be distracted by the need to pee, eat, sleep...

A concrete example was when I was trying to not breathe too loudly, being annoyed by the slight noise of my breath. This would make me breathe less. Which would make my level of energy decrease. Which would leave me with less attention to spare for experiencing the world around me, etc.

To be able to listen with my whole body, I need to take care of its needs **before** I'm already totally distracted from a conversation. Instead of investing the effort to avoid my physical processes, I take a hint, and make sure to deal with them, maintaining my listening device without a big fuss.

The next step was not being disturbed by different flows, but instead being able to relax with them and adapt.

Flow in my definition is a sensation of movement from one area of the body to another or a sensation of activity.

Sometimes I might associate this more with a feeling like fear, anger, love – other times it is merely a physical sensation like a shiver or shaking. When I integrate them as part of my tool to perceive the situation, the drama or automatic need to immediately react reduces. I'm more at ease and again more able to focus on the listening.

Those flows and sensations aren't necessarily **comfortable** – but they are easier to deal with if I don't add the effort of holding something back that I have very limited control over anyway (this is how I explain it to myself at least).

In order to listen, I need a sensation of (enough) time **for impulses to land and be perceived**. When I have that, I can let different impulses be there, and also consider some of those that might be less obvious in the first instance. Being disturbed or needing to react immediately (act, cry, run, answer...) to any sort of physical process makes that impossible. If I am not annoyed by my physical reaction, though, and just act, it is easier for me to notice that some sensations don't necessarily have anything to do with the *story* I'm listening to, but just with my personal maintenance.

If I take care of that personal maintenance by acquainting myself with different physical sensations as well as **relaxing around the fact that I won't be able to control them intentionally all the time**, I can listen more easily. I can notice more easily, which of the flows or sensations are appearing regularly and which are specific to a certain situation. So, which of them is actually giving me information about my present moment and which is a sensation that is actually going on in the background **due to just living**? When I train this by taking time and attention to learn about them in a training setting and paying attention in daily situations, my practice allows me to build trust in my **physical ear**.

During training or while taking this moment of time for listening, it sometimes makes me feel very slow, when I describe all the details I notice like the sensation of cold air passing my skin or of water running down my throat. However, the more regular I keep this practice, the more it actually becomes a skill and I have both strength and fine motor skills in moments, where I need to be fast or effective (think fast, understand fast or act fast). Being able to then also use my whole body and not always taking the **detour around finding a logical explanation**, gives me a much deeper understanding of a situation.

To give you a concrete example: After I slipped on the stairs in my house, I could just stand up, move on as if nothing happened and hope that was the end of it. However, *I know* that falling unexpectedly, especially on the tiny steep stairs, actually gives a moment of surprise and shock. Hitting the spine in the lower end can both hurt that end and the other one (yes – the head). When I'm true to my practice though, I take a moment to lie down, **breathing and noticing** the sensations in my body after this fall – allowing myself to shake for a moment, to move out of the sudden contraction and allowing the moment of fear that comes and goes. It took three-five minutes, and I could feel that my breathing was relaxed, my head didn't create a headache but the throbbing sensation actually diminished, my tailbone was fine, and there was flow going down to my right leg. I noticed that I hit my right foot harder to the ground than I thought and there would probably be a bruise on my heel. The next couple of days I might notice this foot more, and I would take care to relax the leg once in a while, intentionally supporting the flow towards that heel.

Sometimes listening to a situation allows me to say yes or no **before** I know a logical explanation for this choice. It could be called gut-feeling. But sometimes I don't experience it in the guts, either. Sometimes there is just a sudden sensation, **a question**. It could be in the legs. It could be a blurred sensation that, when I pay attention more closely, comes from the layer in between my skin and my muscles.

I train this also by taking moments of listening **to** the body and choosing to give time for the body to work after situations that were intense (sport, emotional situations, worldnews): Lying down and just breathing and noticing what is happening in the body in connection with thoughts or feelings, I learn to interpret the effect of these impulses on my body. Where there is tension, I let it go. Where there is pain, I bring attention and breathe. I let it shake, sweat, shiver... Whatever process is necessary to digest the experience. Sometimes once is enough. Sometimes daily over three months still seems relevant. When I give myself time and space like this, to intentionally notice the body working after intense situations or experiences, I train my ability to **connect a physical sensation with an impulse**. I also feel that when these processes get a space in this way they don't interfere with other, new experiences so much – and I am less disturbed.

I practice this in any activity I do when there is time (or if it is important, I make time) – allowing sensations and impulses **to come to my awareness** rather than searching for and analyzing them. Being open to the possibility that I will receive information through the rest of my body and including the eyes/ears/hands, makes it much easier to still **focus on the activity I'm involved in** at any time. I make a decision about what to focus on as well as staying open to the possibility that I will be influenced passively. This means I sometimes need to allow a great deal of uncertainty, relaxing in situations I cannot control. Not knowing what will come and still relaxing my belly and face, breathing fully and be with the waves of feelings that might come.

Then, since I have trained to relax to be with these flows, I can continue with my budgeting or my conversation with a friend. I can stop up to listen for a moment, if something catches my attention. If, for example, I notice that I'm becoming anxious while I'm taking care of my budget, I can pay attention to this fear and notice whether it comes from an actual tricky situation (e.g. I made a mistake that might lead to a big additional tax payment unless I fix it now) – or if it is an old feeling of insecurity because I am not used to doing this activity. As long as the feeling bothers me and requires attention, it can be disruptive.

So, I can choose to either ignore it – make it numb, push past it (and deal with the consequences later) – or **give it my full attention until the issue is actually dealt with** (the mistake is fixed, or the old wave is over) and doesn't continue to create noise in my mind.

In a way, I think listening with the whole body is the *activity* that finally leads to a sensation of presence. Both on stage, in silent moments or in everyday life. It is a moment of taking as many impulses and impressions in as I can, allowing them to settle and then responding based on a full experience.

And while this sounds like a very slow process – and at times it can be slowing down the immediate reaction – I experience myself to be faster, more accurate, and more comfortable in my interactions with people. Finding more options for solving and changing a situation or connecting with others than when I try to *think myself* to a solution or wait for **things to just happen**.

BASIC QUALITIES

I experience a few basic qualities to be part of the feeling of presence. These basic qualities are both something I see potentially in any living being, and I experience to be strengthened through my practice for Everyday Presence.

In a way, what I call basic qualities are four ways of dealing with feelings and *being* in the aforementioned discomfort. I can strengthen all of these qualities through simply paying attention to the subject or through intentional abstract physical exercises, i.e. working with patterns or isolation. And I find them strengthened through experiences of real life – of exposing myself to situations where I need them. Any practice is still a practice in a somewhat safe space, and **I need the messy, unpredictable space outside** of the practice as well to learn to really trust my experience. That's where I employ these qualities...

COURAGE

Courage is a quality that I need in order to deal with fear.

It may look quite diverse and it can also feel quite differently, but basically, I need it when I enter a new situation or an unknown field. It is what I need, to talk to people about issues that feel vulnerable and important. Or regarding a field where I have a lot of expectations. Or when I have something important to lose and risk it anyway.

Courage appears for me when there is **something more important than the fear of failure**, of getting hurt or needing to look good. It does not take away the fear, but it enables me, to continue pursuing the vision or the issue that is more important, despite the fear.

To be courageous I need to have energy, I need to be able to breathe and move and access my determination so that I won't give up. I need courage to be sure that I gave all I had, all of myself, in the pursuit of what I wanted, while paying attention to life around me as well. Sometimes this could just mean not repeating myself and finding a new solution, thus changing the routine that I had developed to make me feel safe.

I think **courage is a very personal experience**. Being used to move a lot, travel and change apartments, it required much more courage of me to decide to stay in one place and settle there than to move to yet another country or city. Courage means that I notice the fears that are related to this decision (becoming boring, or bored, missing out on something exciting elsewhere) yet simultaneously remembering why I made the decision (wanting to create sustainability, curiosity of what happens when I explore a place longer, boredom of being the new one...).

To do this, I need to breathe and I need to move or dance with my body, otherwise I get restless. In this way, though, **courage makes me energetic and very awake**. I need to pay attention that I do explore the new, the exciting and slightly dangerous – and to use my fear to honestly notice whether any of my worries come true and if so, how to deal with that (am I really bored? How can I unbore myself and still create a stable base?).

I have sometimes mistaken denial for courage and only noticed much later that they are different.

In denial, I would ignore that I am afraid of anything and just focus on my new decision. I would **fake it till I make it**, not listen to my own concerns, pretend that I wasn't scared, and that what I do would not have any effect on others around me. That there would be no risk of losing someone, getting hurt, hurting or creating some kind of embarrassment. But in denial, I feel the level of energy reduce over time. It feels like I need to use my energy in some way, to not feel those fears. For me, it is a cold feeling. Very smooth and slick. I might not intentionally scare or harm others – but by trying to overcome fears or actual danger by pretending to not be touched, I might push people away or hurt them otherwise... It can feel very fast and like I am trying to push past a feeling or thoughts that would otherwise interrupt the slickness. For denial, I stop breathing and I control my movement. I need to make an effort and push through, to not feel the pain that might be caused, the doubt or the embarrassment that is included in the situation.

When I experience courage, it doesn't feel smooth most of the time. It is bumpy and my whole body is involved in a kind of shaking (this can be very subtle or actually visible, depending on the intensity of the moment). I breathe intentionally in a way that keeps me awake and, I focus on feeling my legs on the ground. And I am not speaking metaphorically here – **I really focus on feeling my legs**. In times when things are particularly exciting and challenging, I do exercises to notice my legs and pelvis more clearly (exercises from dancing, from body attention training or climbing, depending on the mood and the day). I then use the energy I get from these physical experiences to focus and notice what is going on around me. Notice the effect of the courageous act on the people involved, on the world around me and on myself. And often this brings exciting new experiences.

Sometimes I regret. I feel my venture was probably a dumb idea after all. Or I will have to say sorry to someone I care about if they were involved. But this certainly gives me a rich and interesting experience of life.

For me, courage means to keep breathing, to keep moving. To go for something unexpected and take a chance when there is something I believe in or am curious about. To be vulnerable to the fact that **I might just have made a stupid mistake** and my life might change forever. Even in a tiny way. Something that I didn't anticipate might happen.

With courage, I feel a certain level of tension or maybe just excitement in my body. There is something I'm afraid of and instead of letting this keep me from exploring and performing, **I stay awake**. I use the fear to pay attention, to notice if there is actually something that might be dangerous and that I should be careful about, or if there are certain consequences of my actions that I'll have to deal with. And then I'll try to use the energy of the fear of failing to deal with those consequences.

I consider courage to be a quality that maintains my sense of humor and laughter when it gets tough. It helps me when I'm being honest with my mistakes, my pain or my fear, to continue exploring the moment and, through laughing, seeing the situation in a larger context and possibly also in its absurdity.

Or is it the other way around? Does my sense of humor allow me to be more courageous, by taking away the heaviness of my self-importance (that can be connected to worry and suffering) and instead taking a more playful approach to the situation?

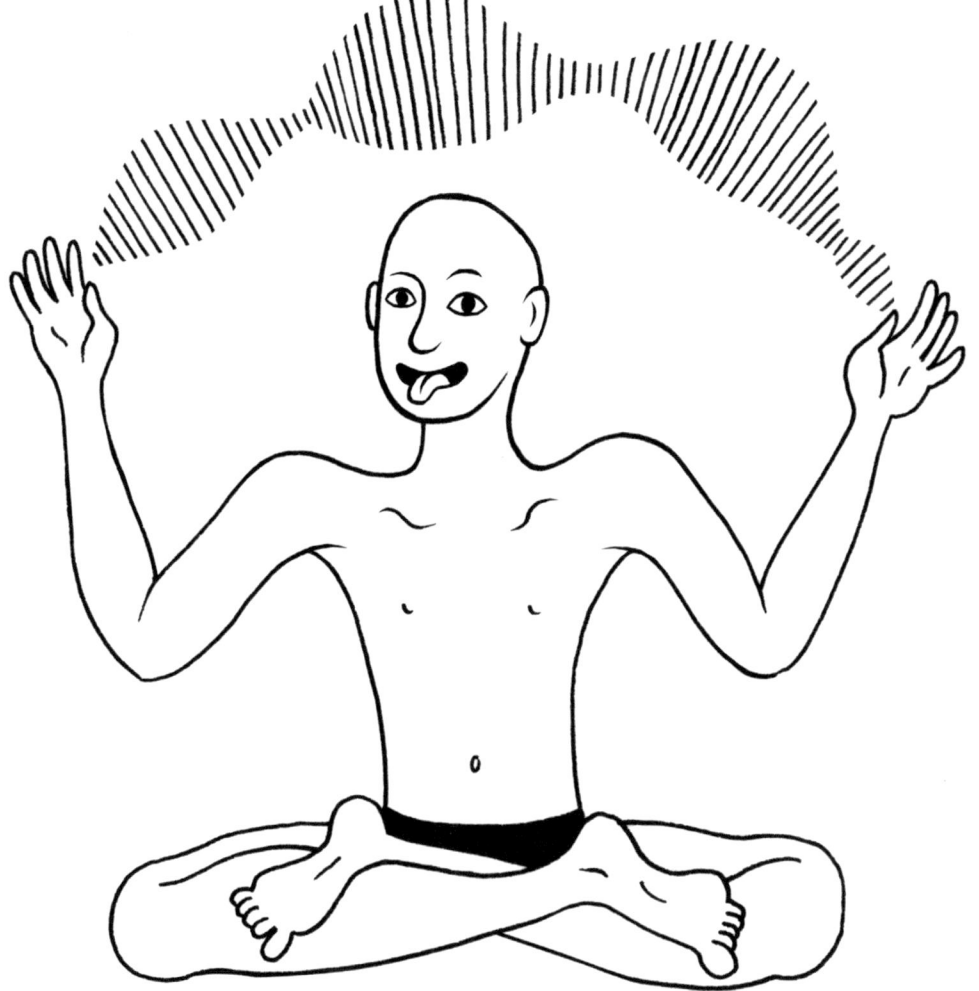

CONFIDENCE

Confidence is a calmer sensation for me. It is very stable, or rather undramatic.

Confidence for me is a basic trust that **I can deal with what will happen**. It doesn't matter whether I know the situation in advance or if I am entering unknown territory, whether I'll do something perfectly or I'll fail. I trust that I will be able to deal with the consequences. That means I know I will be able to deal with both success and pain. I will find a way to continue life and not be destroyed, limited, or repressed by doubt.

When I am courageous and do things that I find important (or interesting, close to my heart) despite the fact that I might look stupid, fail or get freakishly hurt, and I find out that I managed to deal with it, I strengthen my confidence. When I'm confident, it is much easier to seize those moments and jump into something unknown, be courageous.

Confidence comes from experiencing that this is true. From being in challenging situations and experiencing that I manage to deal with them. From learning a new skill and noticing that I'm able to learn it. From adapting something in a new situation, integrating all my experience and using it in any situation. And also, confidence comes from learning to notice my body and my needs.

I notice that it is easier to be both courageous and confident when my basic physical needs are satisfied. When my perceived energy has a basic **level** and I can actually focus on other things besides survival. When I notice physically that I can deal with a situation, my confidence in this, my trust, is much stronger.

When I haven't slept enough or eaten well, when I'm actually stressed out and have used all of my resources just to survive the day without collapsing, an unexpected question or a meeting with someone I'm very impressed by, can suddenly make me doubt and thus shake my confidence.

Discovering the **physical aspect of confidence** was really life changing, to me. To notice that I am irritable (which I might have associated with feeling insecure and needing to stand my ground before) in situations when I'm actually hungry really made a change. (In the mean time I also learned the term hangry...) This discovery also leads to more confidence when I'm hungry both because I can notice that this is what it's about, and because I don't need to defend myself. And it leads to more energy because I can use my irritation as a signal to remember taking a break and taking care of my nutrition. In many situations, this knowledge has led to less doubt and a more clear process of thinking – ok, what do I need in order to deal with the consequences of these actions successfully?

Instead of making me feel stuck and incapable, insecurity now offers me a reminder to think and find out, what else I might need to take care of (basic needs, conversations with others, skills I need to learn), in order to build the courage and confidence to deal with what is coming.

Sometimes I confused self-righteousness with confidence. The sensation, that I am **right** in how I deal with things, what I say and do. And with it the need for others to confirm that I am right, or I might judge them to be *just stupid* or not as smart as me or trying to crush me. When I'm self-righteous, I cannot stand to make a mistake and someone sees it, because the value of myself is somehow connected to being *right*. **When I'm confident**, on the other hand, these two things are not connected. **Others' approval is irrelevant** in that my experience is my experience, and no one needs to confirm my experience for it to be true. I can confidently make a mistake and know that the value of my person is not in question. **Because I trust**, that if I were to make a mistake, I would find out how to fix it, learn from it, or possibly deal with the pain.

When I am confident, I do care about what others think, too, because I am interested in their perception and in learning new things. Their experience adds to mine and gives a more complete picture. But I don't need their **approval** to trust my own experience.

And it is my decision, how much of theirs I want to integrate into my own assessment of the situation.

When I'm confident, I also don't need to be original. It is enough for me to notice that this is **me**. That something is good for me and my world – I don't need to have invented it or to be better than others. I don't need to have traveled to all the countries of the world – currently, I just want to arrive here and have more time to explore.

For me, both denial and self-righteousness are connected to a painful pride. Not the pride of having achieved something, the fleeting happy feeling of „look what I've done! Yeah!" Rather, the kind of pride that is actually hurtful, of pretending to be better than others or in some way above them. The pride that compares my experiences and achievements to that of others, rather than just valuing what I have.

Confidence and courage are both very powerful yet humble sensations. To live them is constantly exciting and relaxing – a fine line of change that I can sometimes trip over and stumble, and sometimes just enjoy.

With courage, I seek out unknown or otherwise uncertain situations to experience something new and widen my window of perception. With confidence, I rest with my experience being my experience. It is neither wrong nor right, but it is mine. Both of them give me an entrance to and are results of a sensation of being present – in everyday life or else.

CLARITY

Clarity to me is a combination of being able to notice a large context and focusing this larger experience on a specific subject.

When I am present in everyday moments, listening with the whole body, honest about what I am perceiving and curious of how the situation will develop, clarity is the ability to prioritize which impulse is essential for me to follow in order to be present and not to feel overwhelmed.

I have been there. Believing that I want to give everything, hear everything, listen to everyone and solve all problems. Not only am I being megalomaniac to imply that all of this responsibility could be mine and that basically, others around me wouldn't be able to do any of the important stuff – I also exhaust myself to a point where I end up crushed. Any activity suddenly feels like its success is crucial to my survival, while it actually has nothing to do with what I am trying to deal with at the moment. I really just need to rest and select, to gain energy. *These* are relevant for my survival.

Even when I just focus on traditional ways of perception with the eyes, for example, I have to select in order to be able to see anything. I cannot see everything. **I have to decide – intentionally, unconsciously or randomly** – on a direction, a range of focus. I also need to be experienced in interpreting the things I see, or they will mostly be colors and shapes. And even with a trained eye, when I come to a new place or see something that I don't know, it might start with being just colors and shapes to me. Or when I want to take in everything that reaches my eyes at once, it becomes more or less blurry. I can still see movement, directions and colors but fewer details. The same is true for listening with the whole body. Perceiving with the whole body, I also **need to focus my attention** to perceive clearly.

When I can't concentrate on what I set out to focus on (a conversation, a song...), my ability to be present is distracted. However, if I follow this distraction for a moment and focus on that, as it in some way seems to be important, **I figure out what is pulling my attention away** and where to. Then I check if this is something I want or need to take care of and how urgent it is –

> is it something I just need to write down and remember for later, in order to be present in the current situation?

> Is it so urgent that I need to do it now?

> Is it a habit and in fact I just need to dare experiencing the feeling of missing something very important while focusing on the thing I actually want to focus on?

Following the wish to practice presence, I can use the sensation of clarity (or its absence) to navigate in moments when I'm in doubt. Clarity is a sensation of being in direct connection with reality. There is no question, what hurts, what I want, or where I need to find an answer. There are new questions – of how to take care of things, how to move on, but they are appearing in a space where thinking is possible. Where feelings, facts, and relations can be perceived at the same time and create the base for the next step. While clarity is a calm sensation, it also **enables me to be quick and clear** with my communication or other interactions.

I experience clarity when I move beyond the fear of missing out on something or of focusing on the wrong thing. It emerges when I allow myself to fully notice the moment in its complexity and with the intention to connect with whatever is going on around me.

The more I am able to listen with the body, the more I perceive clarity as a physical experience when something makes sense or is finished. There is a sense of understanding or peace of mind in it, which allows me to use my current situation as a base to build on and take the next steps.

MUSICALITY

Musicality is a quality beyond right and wrong. Instead, there is a sensation of playing and dancing in life.

In dancing, it is my personal interpretation of the music – in velocity, acceleration, size, and intensity of a movement – and using my trained skills in combination with my interpretation of the other impulses I get (from a partner, the space I'm in, the particular clothes I'm wearing). It is the mix of my conscious decisions about which skills and movements I want to engage, and random things that happen which I then integrate.

When I play an instrument, musicality is the application of my skills – breath, fingers, arms, whatever else I need there – and my interpretation of the instructions plus coincidence and play. My decisions about which notes to emphasize, which breaks to hold, where to do double tempo or improvise freely.

Which emotions might be triggered or also which mood I start with, will influence my play. And while this is possible with any kind of music, there may be certain genres that inspire me more to be free. Why that is, is not really traceable, or might have to do with my entire life and upbringing as well as random encounters, injuries, and training. There are also some dancers with whom it is easier for me to be musical, and others where I feel more inspired to focus on technique and use the dance as training.

I experience musicality as a quality involving the whole body. Rather than being particularly focused on hearing, I find it to be a quality of movement. **Maybe the pendant to listening with the whole body in terms of expression?**

In a way, it is what adds the art to any activity. It makes a dance a dance rather than a set of steps. It makes a piece of music a piece of music rather than a set of sounds heard consecutively.

And as I define it in this way, I realize that this quality adds a

sensation of pleasure and flow to any area of my life that comes from the combination of the activities going on with my way of being present in them.

There are moments of frustration, of fighting, of desperation where nothing seems to fit together. But when I remember this quality of musicality and can employ it, it can be present even when I engage in procrastinating activities or struggle with an unpleasant email. I can experience it in a painful period of time when I have been hurt, am angry or just don't know what to do.

When I do things in my own time, my own order, my own rhythm – when I practice relaxing into my experience of the moment and applying skills and qualities from all of me – it can be a musical experience, and I stop suffering. It opens the option of doing things slower – or faster – than the average or official pace, and to find my own way. It opens the option of a moment of waiting to be a moment of emphasis or preparation. Of raising energy for the moment right after by creating anticipation and curiosity. It opens the option of **adapting subjects or skills from a formerly unrelated area of life**. And like turning a broken teapot into a lamp, I can repurpose the skills I learned when being bored in school (developing my writing messages to my friend without looking at my hand, looking straight ahead at my teacher) – into the practice of touch-typing while looking at my screen. I can switch between keeping a regular structure and improvising my time plan when there is space for it. I can repeat a phrase or activity and notice how it differs the second time around.

Sometimes I find it helpful to have a basic structure within which I move freely. So just like there are basic steps in a specific dance that I can fall back on when I need to catch myself, I may make decisions to create a basic timeframe within which I move during the week. Or I give myself a deadline for when I want to be done with a project like this book. This gives me a frame to move within – and some days I work more, some less. My mood on one particular day might add a different quality or sensation to the process of writing and thinking than on another day. And in the end, I might finish before or after the deadline. But if I am in doubt, the frame that I committed to gives me something to fall back to. **And anything that happens in between is part of the music, part of the dance**. Then I can adapt my skills, twist them, play with the **raw material** that I meet and create a new moment.

And I love being able to change that structure from time to time. Sometimes it is **my choice**, at other times it is something outside of me that initiates this change.

When I employ courage by committing to a certain decision and musicality, it becomes an opportunity for a new dance, a new meal, a new encounter, a new aspect in the aesthetics of my life.

EPILOGUE: PRESENCE EVERY DAY

At the age of 21 I was in Tel Aviv for the first time, and I was scared before that – because I knew I was going to one of these places, where you could be a victim of a bomb attack. One evening, my local friends invited me to a beach party. It was one of the best parties I have ever been to. While I was still afraid, what might happen, there was a strong spirit of life and joy. The atmosphere and attitude there seemed to be „we might die tomorrow, so let's enjoy while we can".

That sounds trivial and like I've heard it many places before. But there on that beach, I **felt** it for the first time.

Since I was 16, I have known people living in areas with possible bombings or other kinds of horrible events. And any time I hear of a new one of those, I worry. I contact them when possible. I make sure that they are still alive. And so far I have been lucky – no one I knew has died in this way. But many have been hurt, many have lost someone they loved or knew. Many are subject to the terror and the fear of not knowing when it will happen.

Since then, there have been more bombings and shootings in places where I know people. And even more in places, where I don't know anyone. The shooting in Paris in 2015 was one of those horrible, unsettling moments. And at the same time, it was no worse than what has happened before. But it has come closer to where I live. Last year, it came to Berlin... I know more people there. I contacted them to know if they were alive, and I'm still lucky – we all are.

Since then, I have experienced a kind of silence inside.

Like so many times before, I didn't know what to do, what to say, I only felt the overwhelming sense of loss, of confusion, and at the same time of love for life.

Overwhelming events can provoke powerlessness, as it seems that the world needs to change for something to be done about it. Because there isn't just Paris, there are also all the other places where things are going wrong. Where people die. Somehow since that Friday in November 2015 I feel a similar sensation to what was there in Tel Aviv. I want to enjoy every moment as much as I can, while I can. And even though it sounds so cliché, I want to be in touch with the people I care about and value our interactions while I can.

I want to hear music, I want to dance, I want to laugh and see art. I want to touch. I want to show people around me how they can be afraid without making themselves small but instead grow anyway, enjoy anyway. How they can mourn and feel the intensity of any feeling without being powerless, but instead being able to notice the love as well. How not to be overwhelmed, but *to contain* the paradox feelings that exist and have the power to create the changes they see are needed in their community. To notice the excitement of life. Of still being here, not giving in to the threat that death seems to be.

I want to allow the silence that follows the storm.

The silence that is full of pain and fear and not knowing what is going to happen. And **I want to move in it and see**.

People. Humans. Life.

This is to the world.

This is to Life.

Thank you

Emma Ekstam for the beautiful illustrations in this book. When you said YES to working with me on this, the book suddenly turned from a dream into a project. And what a beautiful one. I am honored and humbled by the beauty of your images.

Amy Scott for your questions and comments in the process of developmental editing. Sharing my words with a stranger who professionally works with words felt so vulnerable. Your professional, yet personal approach allowed me to look beyond my initial thoughts and create something more coherent.

Marie for being an inspiration to just go and write a book about something you care for. I learned so much following your process and was happy to have a friend *who knows* when I attempted this.

Alexander, Aman, Mascha, Julia, and Cheryl for your time and patience in reading and commenting as my first readers. Thank you for your kindness and support as well as your bullshit-sniffing and disagreement.

Katrine for offering your language-nerd Eyes to check grammar language and commas,,,,...

All my friends, colleagues and clients who have engaged in conversations with me and allowed me to move forward in exploring these subjects.

Laura, Mama und Papa. Darum.

You, dear reader. I am thrilled that you got all the way to this page.

Thank you for your attention.

APPENDIX

Inspiring Resources about the Body, Attention, Living

Here is the beginning of a list that will probably go on forever. Books, podcasts, videos that I enjoy to think about, try out, exercise with, laugh about. It is impossible to make a comprehensive list of everything that has been important to me. However, I want to share some, as a starter for your curiosity. At the end you will find a link to my website where this list will be continued as I stumble over more references.

Somatic Exercises

Body and Earth http://www.body-earth.org/work

How to Sit in Meditation https://soundcloud.com/mindfulmagazine/the-mindful-practice-podcast-how-to-sit-in-meditation

Different Guided Body Attention Exercises I give to clients and also practice myself https://soundcloud.com/ninia-schwan/

Conversations (Podcast, Blog,...)

The Liberated Body Podcast with Brooke Thomas.

Embodied Cognition and Health with Cathy Kerr http://www.liberatedbody.com/cathy-kerr-lbp-056/

Your Body is Your Soul, Jaap van der Wal http://www.liberatedbody.com/jaap-van-der-wal-lbp-057/

Our Relationship to Our Bodies and Their Relationship to the World, Judith Aston http://www.liberatedbody.com/judith-aston-lbp-034/

On Being Podcast with Krista Tippett http://onbeing.org/

About Pain https://painisreallystrange.wordpress.com/

Sophia Davis' Blog http://sophiadavis.de/questioning-the-science-of-mind-body-interactions/

Seth Godin's Blog http://sethgodin.typepad.com/

Katrin Müller's Blog http://beautyandthebananaskinsofbeing.com/

Books I Enjoyed and Find Related (Body, Mind, Being, Knowing...)

Hanna, Thomas: Somatics: Reawakening the Mind's Control of Movement, Flexibility, and Health

van der Kolk, Bessel: The Body Keeps the Score: Brain, Mind, and Body in the Healing of Trauma

Juhan, Deane: Job's body

Noë, Alva: Out of Our Heads

Noë, Alva: Action in Perception

Holmes, Jamie: The Power of Not Knowing

Langer, Ellen J.: Mindfulness

Carse, James P.: Finite and Infinite Games

Kleon, Austin: Steal like an Artist

Pratchett, Terry: I Shall Wear Midnight (And his other Discworld-Novels. Wonderful and funny descriptions of life!)

To be continued here: www.aninia.dk/inspiring-resources-body-attention-living

Movement Practices I have engaged in...

By now you may have realized that I love movement. And I am curious about exploring different forms of movement, both because it is fun and because I am curious about what I can do with my body. Here is a non-comprehensive list of forms of movement I have practiced so far. Where I have added time, it means I did it extensively in this period. Other movement practices have been less regularly or less frequent try out (but more than just once or twice).

My own free dance – since forever until now

Gymnastics (I don't remember... I think I was 8-10 years old and did it for 1 year)

Flamenco (1994-1995... didn't get quite as good as her https://www.youtube.com/watch?v=vjeMg1C-Nv4)

Eurythmie (ca.1987-2001... maybe that's where my need for weird movements started? and my aversion to hippy–dippy-veils? https://www.youtube.com/watch?v=upT5it63f-I)

Ballroom dancing (1996-1997)

Volleyball (1996-2002 https://www.youtube.com/watch?v=Qv1mA1s8p9Y)

Cello (1990-2005 https://www.youtube.com/watch?v=MTveMR0wxT0)

Skiing (1993-2005 ca. once a year https://www.youtube.com/watch?v=Ek9yw4JdEF0)

Singing (2007-2008)

Grinberg Method® Movement Training (2008-now https://www.youtube.com/watch?v=IJsfwuf6-Ao)

Modern Dance (2007-now)

Contact Impro (2007-2009 https://www.youtube.com/watch?v=H8JiB2Nv5Qo)

ImproTheater (2007-2009 https://www.youtube.com/watch?v=ttMLJYkIZGk)

Mask Theatre (2009, 2016 https://www.youtube.com/watch?v=zlNfaYRTzAY)

Capoeira (2010-2011 https://www.youtube.com/watch?v=Z8xxgFpK-NM)

Nia (2010-2011 https://nianow.com/)

Body-SDS Training (2012 https://www.body-sds.dk/en/)

Swingdances (Lindy Hop, Balboa, Blues 2012-now
https://www.youtube.com/watch?v=pyGwN3NNEM0)

Fusion (2015-now https://www.youtube.com/watch?v=znuDuxmaaZU)

Climbing (2013-2015...inspiration and ambition... nowhere near Yosemite
for me, but FUN challenges! https://www.youtube.com/watch?v=l_lZc7nATT4)

Saxophone (2014, 2017)

AkroYoga (2015-2016 https://www.youtube.com/watch?v=W3ENHNlXRfg)

Gaga (2013, 2016-now http://gagapeople.com/english/)

Running (2016-now)

Hiking

About Aninia:

Born 1983. Grew up in Berlin. Moved to Copenhagen in 2012.

After working in theatre, youth empowerment, and creative leadership I wanted to get closer to the body. And I did:

Since 2009 working intensely with people and their bodies. I enjoy my practice of teaching people tools to connect the mind- and physical experiences in their lives. www.aninia.dk

Through this and my personal curiosity I found writing in 2015. https://allinmybody.wordpress.com/

And rediscovered playing with masks in 2016: https://www.instagram.com/sillyfaces.uncoveringmasks/

Life is Movement. Life is Play. Life is a Dance with so many exciting things.